Welcome

Welcome to the FOURTEENTH edition of *loca*
for purchasing this copy. We are delighted by the response from both readers and
participating establishments which has shown a significant increase in both areas.

The purpose of this guide is embodied in the title. Some years ago, we felt that local
people (such as ourselves) or visitors had very little quality information regarding
places serving food and drink. Furthermore, we felt that there was a genuine need
for a specialist book to cover just the catering industry on a local basis. So *local
Food And Drink* was born. We want it to be very much *your* guide about *your*
local food and drink outlets. It is imperative, therefore, that you continue to advise
us as to your likes and dislikes regarding our various publications.

We also urge you to try as many of your local establishments as possible because
without your continued support the choice of venues in your surrounding area will
diminish. **So go on try somewhere new!**

Happy eating and drinking.

Mick Heron

Publisher

Published by Localguides Ltd Byron Lodge, 3 Royston Road, Harston CB2 5PU Tel: 01223 507877. This is not a complete list of eating and
drinking establishments in the region. Inclusion does not imply a recommendation or approval by the publisher. The information in this
guide has been compiled from details supplied by the proprietors of the establishments listed herein. The publisher do not accept liability
for any ommissions from, or inaccuracies, in this publication or for any inconvenience caused thereby.

How to use your guide

Your guide has been carefully designed to be the most functional of its kind in the UK. The tools available to you are:

♦*speed selectors* - allowing you to make an at a glance selection, choosing from 21 facilities and services.

♦*directories* - hundreds of restaurants, pubs, hotels, cafés and takeaways personally visited by our editors and described in full. *Note where a venue has been selected for editor's choice or value for money, a reference will appear on location line.*

♦*editor's choice* - a range of venues favoured by our editorial team.

♦*value for money* - venues that provide very good value for money, usually a place for families.

Contents

Name: *Mark Baker.* **Pub:** *Pemberton Arms, Harston.*
Age: *36.* **Marital Status:** *Engaged, fiancée Vickie.*
Children: *Alex 2 years.*

---

1. **Previous occupation?** *Electrician.*
2. **Why are you a landlord?** *To run my own business and meet people.*
3. **Difference between a tenant and a manager?** *As a tenant whatever efforts I put into the business I get out with job satisfaction and of course remuneration!*
4. **Worst thing about the job:** *The hours.*
5. **Best thing about the job:** *The people that you meet, both good and bad!*
6. **Career ambition:** *To build a single pub to its optimum success level.*
7. **Effect on family life:** *The hours, but at least working from home I see a lot of Alex.*
8. **How do you handle drunks:** *Carefully. And I always wash my hands afterward!*
9. **What do you think of any future smoking ban?** *Long term good, but will probably be an initial downturn, until new customers are attracted into a smoke free atmosphere.*
10. **Do you have a conscience selling a customer too much alcohol?** *Obviously there's a legal obligation plus if I saw someone continually drunk I'd try to have a discreet word.*
12. **What should the legal age be for drinking?** *18. Alcohol is a drug after all.*
13. **How often do you clean your pipes?** *Every week.*
15. **Best experience in the job.** *Leaving party from last pub when we got such positive feeback about the job that we had done.*
16. **Worst experience?** *Any time someone gets excessively drunk, or when trade drops off and you are not sure why!*
17. **What part should a pub play in the community?** *A meeting place, a little like the old days when pubs also housed a post office and a shop.*
18. **Your favourite drink and meal?** *IPA, thats why I keep it so well! Fillet steak.*
19. **Do you support the change in licencing?** *Yes, so that pubs can open at appropriate times for their clientele.*
20. **Any advice to a new landlord?** *You are tied to the business and it's not a job, it's a lifestyle!*
21. **Any hobbies?** *Not much time but when I can, a round of golf and pool and darts of course!*

3

Area 1

Ipswich, Braintree, Halstead, Sudbury, Stowmarket,
Saxmundham, Snape, Aldeburgh, Woodbridge,
Felixtowe, Harwich, Clacton-on-Sea, Colchester
and surrounding areas.

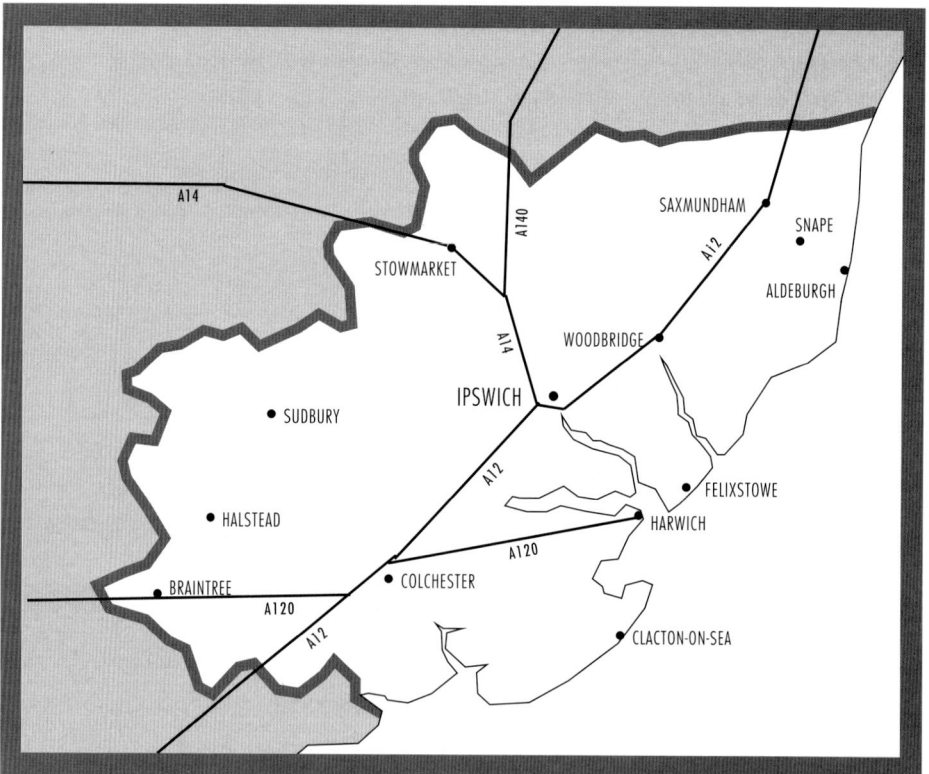

	Disabled Access	No Smoking	Air Conditioning	Coaches Welcome	Live Music	Functions	Credit Cards	Vegetarian Food	No. of Covers	Average Price	Garden	Play Area	Child Portions	Baby Changing	No. Bedrooms	Rooms From £	Real Ales	Takeaway	Pets Welcome	All Day Opening	Waterside Setting	Page No.	Nearest Town
Admirals Head	•			•	•	•	•	•	70	9	•		•				3					9	Woodbridge
Aldeburgh Spice	•			•		•	•	•	26	7	•		•					•		•		9	Aldeburgh
The Alma	•			•			•	•	30	4.50	•		•				3			•		9	Colchester
Angel Inn	•			•	•	•	•	•		4	•		•				2			•		9	Woodbridge
Artillery Man	•			•		•	•	•	50	5	•						2			•		9	Colchester
Barley Mow				•	•	•	•	•	42		•		•		2					•		9	Ipswich
The Bell Inn (1)	•			•		•	•	•	32	8	•		•				2		•	•		10	Braintree
The Bell Inn (2)	•			•			•	•	60	8.50	•		•				3	•	•			10	Hadleigh
Bengal Palace						•	•	•	45	7								•		•		10	Colchester
Bengal Villa R.						•	•	•	56	6								•				10	Sudbury
Bildeston Crown	•			•	•	•	•	•	70	12	•		•	•	10	45	3		•			10	Hadleigh
Black Horse	•			•	•	•	•	•	30	4	•		•				1					10	Sudbury
Blue Boar Hotel	•			•		•	•	•	30	4	•		•				1					11	Colchester
The Boars Head	•		•	•	•	•	•	•	30	4.95	•	•	•				1					11	Braintree
Brewery Tap	•		•	•	•	•	•	•	100	7.50	•	•	•	•			3				•	11	Ipswich
Brittania	•			•		•	•	•	60	5	•		•				3		•			11	Colchester
Bucks Head	•			•		•	•	•	60	6	•	•	•	•			3		•			11	Eye
The Bull at Bacton	•			•	•	•	•	•	48	12	•	•	•									11	Stowmarket
The Bull Inn	•			•		•	•	•	56	9	•		•				3					12	Sudbury
Bumpers F.D.	•					•	•	•	84	5			•					•	•			12	Felixstowe
Clacton Tandoori	•		•	•		•	•	•	42	9								•		•		12	Clacton on Sea
Cork Bar				•	•	•	•	•	60	7	•		•				3		•		•	12	Felixstowe
The Cricketers	•			•	•	•	•	•	25	4	•		•				2		•			12	Braintree
Crystal Charcoal R.	•			•		•	•	•	75	4	•	•						•		•		12	Colchester
The Dog	•			•			•	•	46	7.75	•	•	•				3		•	•		13	Woodbridge
Essex Skipper	•		•	•			•	•	50	8	•		•				2	•	•	•		13	Clacton on Sea
Foresters Arms	•			•		•	•	•	65	10	•		•				2		•			13	Ipswich
Fox & Hounds	•			•		•	•	•	30	5.50	•		•				4	•	•	•		13	Sudbury

5

Name	Disabled Access	No Smoking	Air Conditioning	Coaches Welcome	Live Music	Functions	Credit Cards	Vegetarian Food	No. of Covers	Average Price	Garden	Play Area	Child Portions	Baby Changing	No. Bedrooms	Rooms from £	Real Ales	Takeaway	Pets Welcome	All Day Opening	Waterside Setting	Page No.	Nearest Town
The Fox Inn (1)	•				•	•	•	•	35	8		•	•		1	60	2		•			13	Southwold
The Fox Inn (2)	•			•	•	•	•	•	30	7.50		•	•				3		•			13	Colchester
Grahams on the G.	•	•			•	•	•	•	60	11		•	•	•								14	Chelmsford
Green Man Inn	•	•			•	•	•	•	28	6		•	•				2		•			14	Wickham Market
The Griffin Inn	•			•	•	•	•	•	45	6.90		•	•		3	40	3					14	Saxmundham
Half Butt Inn	•				•	•	•	•	30	5		•	•				4		•			14	Colchester
Henny Swan					•	•	•		60	10	•	•	•				2					14	Sudbury
Honeymoon C.R	•				•		•	•	55	4.50		•			60				•			14	Frinton on Sea
King's Head Inn (1)	•					•	•	•	60	7	•	•	•	3	3		•		•	•	•	15	Woodbridge
King's Head Inn (2)	•	•			•	•	•		32	8		•	•				5				•	15	Halstead
Kohinoor Indian R.	•	•					•	•	50	9								•				15	Sudbury
The Layer Fox	•					•	•	•	58	6.50		•					2					15	Colchester
Lemon's						•	•										1					15	Witham
Lion Inn	•					•	•		50	7		•	•				2		•	•		15	Colchester
The Lord Nelson	•						•												•	•		16	Colchester
Manor Plaice	•	•				•	•	•	40	4								•				16	Braintree
Margaret Catchpole	•			•	•	•	•	•	40	4.50	•	•							•			16	Ipswich
Marlborough Head	•			•	•	•	•	•	78	6		•					3		•			16	Colchester
McDonalds (1)	•	•					•		160	3.25		•	•	•				•				16	Clacton on Sea
McDonalds (2)	•	•					•		50	4	•	•	•					•			•	16	Felixstowe
The Mill Inn	•			•	•	•	•	•	40	9.50	•	•			4	45	3					17	Aldeburgh
Moon & Mushroom	•						•		60	8.95		•					7					17	Ipswich
Monty's Restaurant	•					•	•	•	76	12							2					17	Colchester
Nando's	•					•	•	•	30	6										•		17	Colchester
The Oak	•					•	•	•	50	4		•			3		•		•			17	Stowmarket
The Old Chequers	•					•	•	•	52	8		•					•	•	•			17	Aldeburgh
Old Queen's Head	•					•	•		32	8		•					•	•	•			18	Colchester
Oyster Inn	•					•	•	•	45	8.25		•	•				•	•	•			18	Woodbridge

6

	Nearest Town	Page No.	Waterside Setting	All Day Opening	Pets Welcome	Takeaway	Real Ales	Rooms From £	No. Bedrooms	Baby Changing	Child Portions	Play Area	Garden	Average Price	No. of Covers	Vegetarian Food	Credit Cards	Functions	Live Music	Coaches Welcome	Air Conditioning	No Smoking	Disabled Access
Peacock Inn	Hadleigh	18			•		4		3		•		•	15	65	•	•	•	•	•		•	•
Peldon Rose	Colchester	18		•	•		4	50		•	•		•	10	130	•	•	•	•	•		•	•
Penny's Bar & R.	Ipswich	18												12	80	•	•	•	•	•		•	•
Perfect Kebab H.	Ipswich	18				•					•			3	8	•	•					•	•
Plough & Sail	Woodbridge	19	•			•	5			•	•		•	10.75	120	•	•	•	•	•		•	•
Red Lion	Witham	19					2				•			5	60	•	•	•	•				•
Red Rose Inn	Hadleigh	19			•	•	4				•		•	8	60	•	•	•	•	•		•	•
Rose & Crown	Clacton on Sea	19			•		3				•		•	7.50	50	•	•	•	•	•		•	•
Roxi Restaurant	Colchester	19				•					•			8.50	200	•	•	•	•	•		•	•
Scott's Bar & R.	Ipswich	19								•	•		•	13.50	80	•	•	•	•	•		•	•
Shannon Inn	Ipswich	20			•	•	6				•			7	50	•	•	•	•	•		•	•
Shepherd & Dog	Stowmarket	20		•	•		3				•	•	•	4.95	26	•	•	•	•	•		•	•
Ship Inn	Clacton on Sea	20			•	•	2	32.50	8		•		•	10	50	•	•	•	•	•			•
Sibton White Horse	Saxmundham	20				•	3				•	•	•	13.50	48	•	•	•	•	•		•	•
SIC Szechuan Inn	Manningtree	20				•					•			6.95	85	•	•	•	•	•	•	•	•
Simla Balti House	Colchester	20				•					•			8	52	•	•					•	•
Spice Zone	Halstead	21				•					•			3	40	•	•					•	•
Suffolk Punch	Ipswich	21		•							•	•	•	6.95	40	•	•	•		•		•	•
The Swan Inn (1)	Sudbury	21			•		3	45	2		•		•	7.95	24	•	•	•	•	•		•	•
The Swan Inn (2)	Framlingham	21			•	•	2				•		•		23	•	•	•	•	•		•	•
The Tea Rooms	Walton	21									•			8	160	•	•					•	•
Temptations C.B.	Ipswich	21			•	•					•	•	•	10	40	•	•	•	•	•		•	•
The Three Ashes B.	Braintree	22					1				•			4	34	•	•	•				•	•
Tickle Manor T.R.	Sudbury	22			•						•		•	3	15	•	•					•	•
The Trafalgar	Harwich	22		•	•		2				•			6	32	•	•	•	•	•		•	•
Unique	Clacton on Sea	22		•							•			14	90	•	•					•	•
Vanilla Pod R.	Ipswich	22			•						•			7	100	•	•					•	•
Victoria Inn	Felixstowe	22	•		•	•	3				•		•			•	•	•	•	•		•	•

7

	Waterside Setting	All Day Opening	Pets Welcome	Takeaway	Real Ales	Rooms from £	No. Bedrooms	Baby Changing	Child Portions	Play Area	Garden	Average Price	No. of Covers	Vegetarian Food	Credit Cards	Functions	Live Music	Coaches Welcome	Air Conditioning	No Smoking	Disabled Access	Page No.	Nearest Town
Warwick Arms		•		•	2	25	6			•	•	6	50	•		•	•	•			•	23	Clacton on Sea
Water Lily		•									•											23	Ipswich
Westerfield R.		•			3						•	7	36	•	•	•	•	•		•	•	23	Ipswich
White Horse Inn			•		3	40	2			•	•	6.50	24	•	•	•	•	•		•	•	23	Sudbury
Wig & Fidgett		•	•		2					•	•	3.50	38	•	•	•	•	•		•	•	23	Colchester
Zentral Oriental B.				•						•		12.95	90	•	•	•	•	•	•	•	•	23	Colchester

8

Admirals Head
Sandy Lane
Little Bealings

☎ 01473 625912
Location:

This rustic, C17th free house has a nautical feel to it, along with some Nelson memorabilia and 2 wells! Owners, Rosario and Jazmine D'Angelo serve a delightful menu of modern British food with Italian influences and use specialised ingredients for their creative dishes. Super service and 2 private function rooms. **In the middle of the village.**

Aldeburgh Spice
76 High Street
Aldeburgh

☎ 01728 452000
Location:

You'll find this high quality Indian restaurant in the sleepy Suffolk coastal town of Aldeburgh. A wide variety of dishes are served, from mild and creamy to hot and spicy, with favourites such as chicken Passanda and fish Tikka Mossalla, accompanied with Indian beer. Takeaway available with 10% discount. *On the edge of the centre.*

The Alma
Copford Green
Copford

☎ 01206 210607
Location:

Once a brewery, Colin Phillips has refurbished this friendly, village local. The ales are from Greene King and the food is country cooking at its best, including game in season and home-made steak & kidney pie. The dining room is smoke free and the secure beer garden and raised decking are a delight in the summer. *2 miles rom the A12, centrally located.*

Angel Inn
2 Theatre Street
Woodbridge

☎ 01394 382660
Location:

This friendly, family pub, now run by Colin Dagnall has a pretty and secure garden and a new pool table and jukebox. A nice bar menu of traditional dishes is served, such as fresh baguettes, juicy burgers and Suffolk ham, egg & chips. 2 well kept real ales and 2 newly refurbished guest rooms available. *On the edge of the town centre.*

Artillery Man
54-56 Artillery Street
Colchester

☎ 01206 798024
Location: **(EC P.128)**

Tenant, Derek Williams has retained the friendly atmosphere and not made wholesale changes. He serves IPA and Abbot real ales and wine by the glass and is re-introducing food, with a bar menu and blackboard specials, as well as a fine Sunday lunch. A good family venue, with satellite tv, darts, pool and music. *2 miles southeast of the town centre.*

Barley Mow
Mow Hill
Witnesham

☎ 01473 785395
Location:

This old fashioned pub is now run by Mick Doherty, who has created a warm and friendly atmosphere, enhanced by the wood burning stove in winter. Good, wholesome food is served, such as freshly battered fish & chips and a wonderful roast lunch on Sundays. Nice garden for the summer and a regular quiz night. *On Mow Hill*

The Bell Inn (1)
37 Kynaston Road
Panfield
Nr Braintree
☎ 01376 324641
Location:

A cosy, C16th English pub that maintains the best of English traditions, with real ales, home-made pies and Sunday roasts. New tenants, Graham & Tracey Bedford specialise in fresh fish, with over 8 creative dishes to sample, with everything available to take away. Camping and caravan site and a kids play area too.
Centrally located.

The Bell Inn (2)
The Street
Kersey

☎ 01473 823229
Location:

Set in this picturesque Suffolk village, you'll find this delightful C14th, family run inn. Food is served everyday and is freshly cooked to order. Try medallions of pork in a creamy mustard sauce, fresh fish, vegetable lasagne and a super tapas menu available on Sundays and Mondays. 3 cask conditioned ales too.
In the centre of the village.

Bengal Palace
11 Queen Street
Colchester

☎ 01206 545045
Location: (EC P.115)

Open lunchtimes and evenings, 7 days a week, this delightful restaurant serves authentic Indian cuisine of a high standard. Delights include spiced salmon and lobster dishes, Baltis and vegetable Thali and there's a takeaway service available too. Good service by experienced staff in a lively atmosphere.
Beside the Tourist Information Centre.

Bengal Villa Restaurant
52A North Street
Sudbury

☎ 01787 313733/375083
Location: (EC P.125)

A modern and stylish restaurant that offers authentic Indian cuisine with a vast choice of dishes. Choose mild and creamy curries such as lamb Passanda or hot and spicy options like chicken Jalfrezi. Plenty of dining promotions too and a 10% discount on takeaways or free delivery within 5 miles.
At the top of North Street.

Bildeston Crown
104 High Street
Bildeston

☎ 01449 740510
Location:

Dating to 1529, this fabulous hotel and restaurant has recently been refurbished and now boasts classy, yet comfortable and relaxing surroundings. Enjoy light bar snacks, afternoon teas or superb modern British cuisine like smoked cod with mussell chowder. Marquee and a private dining room for functions.
Close to the Market Square.

Black Horse
21 East Street
Sudbury

☎ 01787 377548
Location:

New landlords, Claire & Peter Wakeman, have completely redecorated yet retained the traditional features of this lovely old pub. They have also introduced traditional English food for the whole family plus a takeaway service is available. Open all day, every day, with entertainment every Saturday night.
On the edge of the town centre.

Blue Boar Hotel
3-7 Kendall Road
Colchester

☎ 01206 792235
Location:

Landlord Gareth Gailey provides a hearty welcome to everyone at his traditional pub. He serves a nice menu of home cooked food from tasty bar snacks to a delicious Sunday lunch for only £4.95. Open all day, there's plenty to do with a quiz every Monday night, regular entertainment, jukebox, pool and darts. ***200 yards from the train station.***

The Boars Head
High Street
Braintree

☎ 01376 32 019
Location:

Mark and Sharon have created a super atmosphere at their C15th town centre pub with convenient car park. They serve home-made food, with excellent barbecues in the summer, and a host of entertainment with a quiz on Wednesdays, karaoke on Thursdays, a DJ on Fridays and live music every Saturday. ***In the heart of the town.***

Brewery Tap
Cliff Quay
Ipswich

☎ 01473 281508
Location: (EC P.118)

Grade II listed, filled with Tolly Brewery memorabilia and set in a super location, overlooking the River Orwell. Good ales which are well kept by Angie Halsey and varied pub food, with something to suit everyone. There's a terrraced garden and seats at the front where you can sup a pint and enjoy lovely views. ***Beside the brewery, overlooking the river.***

Britannia
42 Meyrick Crescent
Colchester

☎ 01206 574391
Location: (V P.230)

New tenants, John and Catherine, are certainly making lots of improvements to this pub located close to the local barracks. They serve traditional English bar food from 12-9pm plus senior citizens can eat lunch for £3.50 and kids have their own menu. A friendly and lively atmosphere with weekly entertainment. ***Close to the barracks.***

Bucks Head
Norwich Road
Thwaite

☎ 01449 766219
Location: (EC P.132)

Now under new and enthusiastic management, this family friendly, traditional English pub serves an excellent standard of food. Delicious barbecue chicken melts, wholesome bangers & mash as well as plenty of vegetarian options. Lovely character, with old beams and magnificent open fires, and a nice garden too. ***On the A140, close to Mendlesham Mast.***

The Bull at Bacton
Church Road
Bacton

☎ 01449 781159
Location:

Recently awarded 'Mid Suffolk Pub of the Month' by CAMRA, this C16th pub serves 3 real ales plus a guest ale served from the cask. The chef is award winning too and he prepares modern English dishes like pork belly, roast partridge, delicious home-made pasta and freshly battered fish & chips. ***1/2 mile from the church.***

The Bull Inn
High Street
Cavendish

☎ 01787 280245
Location: (EC P.120)

Now run by Paul & Lynn, who provide a hearty welcome to their pub that dates back to 1522 and comes complete with a murder story! They serve a nice range of traditional pub food at lunchtime and English dishes with an interesting modern twist in the evening. 3 good real ales and a full selection of spirits. *On the main road through the village.*

Bumpers Family Diner
103-105 Hamilton Road
Felixstowe

☎ 01394 278553
Location:

Newly refurbished, this continental style cafe is expertly run by Caron Symes. She serves a large variety of dishes, home-made from local produce, such as soups, salads, roast beef baps and excellent afternoon teas. Pop in for a relaxing cup of coffee, a light snack or a wholesome lunch, or you can takeaway. *Near the seafront and the town centre.*

Clacton Tandoori
126 Old Road
Clacton on Sea

☎ 01255 224464
Location:

This Indian restaurant has a new name and a new owner! Open lunchtime and evening, 7 days a week, there are some fabulous dishes to try from classic favourites to new creations. There's a free delivery service in the local area and a good selection of drinks, including Indian beers and international wines. *Just off the town centre.*

The Cork Bar
Undercliff Road West
Felixstowe

☎ 01394 283562
Location: (EC P.117)

Named after the Corksand Light ship, this super pub has balconies with excellent sea views. There's a beautiful new restaurant, entirely non-smoking, where you can savour traditional English food from fresh fish & chips to succulent steaks. Live music 3 times a week. Booking advisable. *On the seafront.*

The Cricketers
7 West Street
Coggeshall

☎ 01376 561533
Location:

Open all day, new landlady Lorraine Ingleton offers real English hospitality at this C18th pub. She provides excellent food, served from noon until 10pm, such as home-made chicken curry, beef stew, fresh fish & chips and mouth watering rhubarb crumble. Recently refurbished and with a lovely log fire too. *Just off the town centre.*

Crystal Charcoal Restaurant
49 Saint Botolphs Street
Colchester
☎ 01206 545566
Location:

This is a new concept for Colchester. Mr Ozgurcu and his friendly staff serve Turkish food cooked on a charcoal barbecue whilst you watch, or you can try the more conventional dishes such as Turkish meatballs and Kleftico. A great place to host a function, dine from 11am-10pm, takeaways until 1.30am. *Beside the train station.*

The Dog
The Green
Grundisburgh
Woodbridge
☎ 01473 735267
Location: (EC P.126)

This C18th pub has 2 open fires and is full of antique and period furniture. Superb English food, with a modern twist, such as honey-roast organic salmon with a sweet chilli & ginger dressing. A well priced lunch menu too, 3 well kept real ales and an interesting wine list, specialising in wines from small vineyards. *Opposite the green.*

Essex Skipper
Rochford Way
Frinton on Sea

☎ 01255 673574
Location: (EC P.116)

A dramatically improved venue, where all ages are welcome. The freshest of fish, with smoked haddock wrapped in cured ham, salmon on a bed of sauteed leeks and cod in parsley & cheese sauce, as well as steaks, chicken and vegetarian options. There's a good wine list, real ales and varied live entertainment too. *Beside the Triangle Shopping Centre.*

Foresters Arms
Main Road,
Chelmondiston

☎ 01473 780930
Location:

This lovely pub, adorned with oak beams and open fires, has a friendly atmosphere and everyone is made to feel welcome. The chef prepares quality, freshly cooked food for the Anglo-French style menu, such as stuffed pork fillet, and the Sunday roast, complemented by fine wines and beers is very popular. *In the centre of the village on the B1456.*

Fox & Hounds
Church Street
Groton

☎ 01787 210474
Location: (EC P.120)

You will be amazed by the stunning, countryside views from this delightful pub, now run by Mary Fitzgerald. She serves lovely home-made food with regular changes to the menu. Try Suffolk ham with free-range eggs & chips or mouth watering aubergine & tomato bake. 4 real ales and a boules pitch. *Just a few miles from Sudbury.*

The Fox Inn (1)
Fox Lane
Darsham

☎ 01728 668436
Location:

This friendly, old fashioned pub has a cosy atmosphere with 2 real fires. Brian and Nell have a lovely, changing menu of English and continental style food and there's always fresh fish and a choice of steaks and delicious pasta dishes. Sunday lunch is excellent value at £6.50 and there's a guest bedroom for £60. *Just off the A12, in the centre of the village.*

The Fox Inn (2)
East Road
West Mersea

☎ 01206 383391
Location:

The new owners of this C18th free house have a roaring log fire and a choice of 2 interesting menus. Sample light snacks at lunchtime, like home-made soup, baguettes and jacket potatoes, or try tasty dishes like lamb shank and succulent steaks served from Thursday to Saturday evening. Super Sunday lunch too. *On the east side of the village.*

13

Graham's on the Green
12-14 The Green
Writtle

☎ 01245 422432
Location: (EC P.133)

Newly opened and with a minimalist style, this air conditioned restaurant overlooks the duck pond on the village green and offers fantastic Modern European cuisine. There are regular theme events and seafood evenings, light jazz on Tuesdays and a beautiful, heated patio for alfresco dining.
On the village green. www.grahamsonthegreen.com

Green Man Inn
Woodbridge Road
Tunstall

☎ 01728 688351
Location: (V P.230)

Family run, this traditional free house celebrated its 100th anniversary in August 2004! Open all day for great value food and drinks, with OAP specials from £4.50 for 2 courses and beer at just £2 for most pints, all day on Sundays. This is a friendly, family run venue, for all ages, with darts, pool and petanque.
On the edge of the village, on the B1078.

The Griffin Inn
High Street
Yoxford

☎ 01728 668229
Location: (EC P.116)

A friendly pub where you are surrounded by medieval features including gargoyles and heraldic shields. You can dine on C14th recipes too, such as pumpes and medieval stuffed trout, as well as delights like freshly battered cod with home-made tartar sauce. Now with a supper license and monthly folk music.
On the A1120 in the village centre.

Half Butt Inn
Nayland Road
Great Horkesley

☎ 01206 271202
Location:

Landlord, Daniel Smith, keeps an excellent standard of ales, serving Greene King IPA and 3 regularly changed guests. The public bar boasts Sky tv, pool and darts, whilst in the saloon you can sample good pub grub at lunchtimes, mostly for under £5 a person. Kids are welcome, with smaller portions available.
Centre of the village on the A134.

Henny Swan
Henny Street
Nr Sudbury

☎ 01787 269238
Location:

Set by the Stour, this extensively modernised, C17th venue serves a brasserie menu with delights like Cumberland sausage & mashed potato and slow-roasted lamb shank, prepared by a top chef. A large beer garden sweeps down to the river which boasts patio dining, a new jetty for boats plus a large parking area.
Just off the A131, 2 miles south of Sudbury.

Honeymoon Chinese Restaurant
7 Old Pier Street
Walton on the Naze
☎ 01255 670888
Location: (EC P.122)

A traditional Chinese decor in this lovely seaside restaurant and a fabulous range of Cantonese, Peking & Thai dishes. Try the Sunday buffet and Sunday evening 'eat as much as you like' menu. Take up the fantastic 3 course lunch offer for £6.80. Open 12-2pm and 5.30pm-midnight, kids welcome. Free delivery too.
Right on the seafront.

14

King's Head Inn (1)
Front Street
Orford
Nr Woodbridge
☎ 01394 450271
Location: (EC P.129)

Step back in time at this C13th former smugglers' inn, with its legends of secret tunnels, rustic interior and open fire. Adnams real ales, locally grown vegetables and the Kings Head Seafood Platter, which includes delicious freshly smoked local fish. A truly atmospheric place to stay, with double rooms from £60.
12 miles east of Woodbridge on the B1084, beside the church.

King's Head Inn (2)
The Street
Pebmarsh

☎ 01787 269306
Location: (EC P.129)

Dating back to 1450, this free house is the focal point of the village. New owners, Graham and Jacqueline keep 3 rotating ales and serve an international menu. There are fajitas, fish & chips, pies and wonderful desserts, including locally produced Hadley's ice cream. Pool, darts, quizzes and live music too!
4 miles northeast of Halstead.

Kohinoor Indian Restaurant
Gregory Street
Sudbury
☎ 01787 311322
Location: (EC P.127)

Award winning chef, Mr Abdul Hoque is the new owner of this stylish restaurant and he brings with him an excellent reputation. He prepares classic Indian dishes to a superb standard, that can be washed down with Indian beer, and he offers free delivery within an 8 mile radius if you spend more than £15.
Opposite the Croft & the riverside.

The Layer Fox
Malting Green Road
Layer de la Haye

☎ 01206 738310
Location:

You'll find a wonderful, friendly atmosphere at this 400 year old free house, now owned by John and Linda McComb. Good food such as mixed grills, steaks and lasagne plus 2 well kept real ales. Open all day with country & western music every Friday night, singing competitions and karaoke evenings.
In the centre of the village.

Lennon's the Underground Bar
7 High Street
Great Dunmow
☎ 01371 879969
Location:

Set on 2 levels, this cellar bar has a modern, minimalist style and is adorned with John Lennon memorabilia. Lots going on with entertainment every weekend, such as live bands, tribute artists and DJs, as well as a large screen satellite tv for Sky sports and Premiership Plus. 1 real ale, a good wine list and bottled beers.
Next to the Oxfam shop.

The Lion Inn
Mersea Road
Langenhoe

☎ 01206 735263
Location:

A lovely inn that specialises in fresh fish from The Mersea to Australia! With over 40 fish dishes, there really is something to suit all tastes. New tenants, Douglas and Deborah Kiddle have created a nice and informal ambience and host fantastic summer barbecues in their landscaped garden. Good wines and real ales.
On the B1025, south of Colchester.

The Lord Nelson
134 Hythe Hill
Colchester

☎ 01206 512729
Location:

No food and no children! This is a traditional, town pub where you can enjoy a relaxing drink in an adult environment. Landlady, Angela Thomson has vast experience in the pub trade and has created a friendly atmosphere at her C19th free house. Lord Nelson adorns the walls and you can play pool or darts. *A mile from the town centre.*

The Manor Plaice Chip Shop & Restaurant
22-24 Manor Street
Braintree
☎ 01376 326889
Location: (EC P.130)

Renowned for their fresh fish and chips to take away but you can also eat in and sample cod, skate, haddock, chicken and many other dishes freshly cooked to order. Open 7 days a week from 11am to 10.30pm, you are guaranteed good quality, wholesome food and excellent service from Adnan and Margaret. *Close to the town centre.*

Margaret Catchpole
Cliff Lane
Ipswich

☎ 01473 400206
Location:

One of the few 1930s pub in the area that has remained in its original condition. A lovely backdrop of Holywells Park makes this a delightful venue. Les serves up good pub food that is suitable for all the family, including Sunday lunch as well as takeaways. Functions welcomed. Good disabled access. *Beside Holywells Park, 1 mile east of the town centre.*

Marlborough Head Hotel
Mill Lane
Dedham

☎ 01206 323250
Location:

This listed building dates to the C14th and boasts glorious open fires which you can relax by and enjoy one of the well kept real ales or fine wines. Delicious food too, with super home-made specials for under £5 like liver & bacon and roast turkey. Open all day and with a separate function room for up to 100 people. *In the centre of the village.*

McDonalds (1)
24 Pier Avenue
Clacton on Sea

☎ 01255 436058
Location:

This well established restaurant is now managed by Rick Wheeler who has recently been awarded 'Manager of the Year'. There's a new range of breakfasts on the menu and now plenty of low fat, healthy options, as well as the classic burger meals. Eat at any time - the restaurant opens from 6.30am to 11pm. *Not far from the pier.*

McDonalds (2)
Haven Exchange
Walton Avenue
Felixstowe
☎ 01394 670713
Location:

This popular restaurant is efficiently managed by Rob Butler and is now open from 6.30am until 11pm. The traditional menu is always available yet there are now a growing range of healthy options like toasted deli sandwiches and salads at less than 3% fat. Children love their own menu which comes with a gift. *Near Dock Gate 1.*

16

Directory

The Mill Inn
Market Cross Place
Aldeburgh

☎ 01728 452563
Location: (EC P.124)

This grade II listed pub dates to the C17th, and situated on the seafront, has a fisherman and lifeboat theme throughout. The 4 guest rooms boast fantastic sea views and the full English breakfasts are delicious. The traditional menu utilises fresh, local produce, with fresh fish caught in the sea just 20 yards away! *On the seafront.*

The Moon & Mushroom
High Road
Swilland

☎ 01473 785320
Location:

This unique, C16th free house is an integral part of the local community and was voted 'Local Pub of the Year' by the 'Evening Star'. There's an amazing choice of real ales, all from East Anglian small breweries, and divine food like wholesome casseroles and plum crumble. Pretty patios, with heaters too! *On the edge of the village just off the B1077.*

Monty's Restaurant
9 North Hill
Colchester

☎ 01206 765006/766395
Location: (EC P.130)

The Chhetri family has lots of experience, having been involved in restaurants for 26 years! Originally from Nepal, they serve authentic Nepalese and Indian cuisine in their 400 year old listed building which is tastefully furnished with antiques and original beams. 10% discount on all takeaways. *Half-way down North Hill.*

Nando's Chickenland
11-13 Head Street
Colchester

☎ 01206 760344
Location:

A superb, new restaurant serving the increasingly popular Portuguese cuisine. Open all day, every day, there are plenty of interesting dishes to try, such as the classic chicken Piri Piri, as well as platters to share. Lovely, secluded outside area for dining or drinking Portuguese wines and beers in the summer months. *Near the top of the High Street.*

The Oak
43 Ipswich Street
Stowmarket

☎ 01449 612024
Location:

This pub has the lot, 3 wonderful real ales, one of which is a guest, international food, from traditional English to spicy Thai & Indian creations and bags of entertainment. An excellent venue for Sky Sports on the large tv, and on Thursday evenings and in summer on Sundays there are live rock bands in the garden. *At the top end of the main shopping street.*

The Old Chequers
Aldeburgh Road
Friston

☎ 01728 688270
Location: (EC P.125)

A superb free house, owned by Lynn & Alan Bailey, who boast Adnams real ales and an impressive wine list. Excellent food, with home-made rabbit stew, local pigeon pie and an amazing 'sausage & mash board' featuring 11 types of sausage, 7 varieties of mash and 7 different gravies! OAP 2 course lunch for £6.95. *On the crossroads.*

17

The Old Queen's Head
Ford Street
Aldham

☎ 01206 241584
Location: (EC P.118)

Now run by Julia Spence who has created a new style restaurant with fantastic dishes prepared by a talented chef. The range of fish dishes has increased and there are some unique vegetarian options as well as wholesome favourites like liver & bacon casserole. Lovely log fires and a popular monthly jamming night. *In the centre of the village.*

Oyster Inn
Butley
Nr Orford

☎ 01394 450790
Location: (EC P.119)

This C14th inn, which is set in 2 acres of grounds and boasts 3 log fires, is now run by Stephen Barker. A superb menu of home-made dishes, with fish and game in season the speciality, is served both lunch times and evenings and can be accompanied by well kept real ales. Children will love the aviary. *6 miles east of Woodbridge on the B1064.*

The Peacock Inn
37 The Street
Chelsworth

☎ 01449 740758
Location:

This family run, traditional country inn boasts superb food, fine wine and real ales and good company. Enjoy a relaxing drink by log fires or indulge in roasted cod on a bed of spring onion mash with a caper sauce or tempura of tiger prawns, followed by Grand Marnier and orange creme brulee. Great jazz nights too. *On the main road through the village. www.thepeacockinnchelsworth.co.uk*

Peldon Rose
Mersea Road
Peldon

☎ 01206 735248
Location:

With a marvellous feeling of history and a smugglers' pond in the garden, this 600 year old pub is actually listed in the Domesday book! There's seating for 130, including a conservatory to accommodate 60, where you can enjoy superb, fresh seafood dishes. 'Cask Marque' commended and 3 en suite rooms. *On the B1025, 5 miles south of Colchester.*

Penny's Bar
& Restaurant
10-12 St Nicholas Street
Ipswich
☎ 01473 280433
Location: (EC P.122)

The only Spanish venue in Ipswich where you can choose from a selection of outstanding tapas as well as a full English menu from light bites to steaks. Food is available all day until 10pm plus there's a good range of drinks, including San Miguel and Sangria! Enjoy Salsa on Mondays and live music on Thursdays. *200 yards from Ipswich Marina.*

The Perfect Kebab
House & Takeaway
20 Falcon Street
Ipswich
☎ 01473 288099
Location:

A good quality takeaway outlet with a highly efficient delivery service, which is free of charge on all orders of £7 or more within a 6 mile radius. Open Sunday to Thursday noon till midnight and Friday to Saturday noon to 3am, choose from a variety of kebabs, burgers, southern fried chicken and of course, chips! *In the town centre.*

The Plough & Sail
Snape Maltings
Snape

☎ 01728 688413
Location: **(EC P.123)**

This lovely venue has a spacious and airy feeling, whilst retaining the rustic charm of the building. A modern English menu, with fresh fish featuring prominently, complemented by a very fine wine list. A thoroughly relaxing place in which to enjoy great food and equally lovely views.
On the Maltings.

Red Lion
Newland Street
Witham

☎ 01376 512199
Location: **(EC P.127)**

A lovely, high street pub that was formerly 'The Black Boy' in the C18th where cock fighting took place. Excellent food with home-made cooking such as all day breakfasts, steak & kidney pie and a great Sunday roast, plus you can dine alfresco on the patio. A friendly atmosphere, ideal for the whole family.
On the edge of Witham town.

Red Rose Inn
The Street
Lindsey

☎ 01449 741424
Location: **(EC P.115)**

This beautiful, C15th coaching inn retains its original beams and inglenook fireplace and is now under new ownership. It boasts an internal play area for the kids and a pets corner in the secure garden, featuring pot bellied pigs! Delightful menu from snacks to medallions of monkfish, 4 real ales and over 50 cocktails.
On the edge of the village.

Rose & Crown
High Street
Thorpe Le Soken

☎ 01255 861525
Location:

Everyone is welcome at this delightful, C17th free house, now owned by Natasha and Campbell. They have introduced a new menu, from fresh sandwiches and hoffers to traditional English fayre like home-made pies, and now serve 3 real ales and a good number of interesting wines - enjoy a glass on the new decking!
On the B1033, in the village centre.

Roxi Restaurant
118 High Street
Colchester

☎ 01206 578569
Location: **(EC P.121)**

This modern ground floor and cellar restaurant serves a good selection of both English and Mediterranean food from 9am until late. Choose delights such as fresh fish and mixed Mezza, or from the changing daily specials menu. Nice patio for alfresco dining, as well as live entertainment and regular theme nights.
Close to the Hippodrome.

Scott's Bar
& Restaurant
4A Orwell Place
Ipswich
☎ 01473 230254
Location:

This family owned restaurant, now with air-conditioning, has a fantastic menu of contemporary dishes, all home-made and freshly prepared. Choose from delights such as roasted minted lamb rump and pan fried sea bass with crayfish mashed potato, as well as a super traditional roast on Sunday lunchtimes.
Near the car park.

19

Shannon Inn
Main Road
Bucklesham

☎ 01473 659275
Location:

Originally 3 cottages, this mid C17th inn offers imaginative dishes such as wild mushroom ravioli, home-made sausages and plenty of fresh seafood. New tenants, Paul & Charlotte Freeman have gained a 'Cask Marque' award for the quality of their 6 real ales and the variety of unusual bitters that they have to offer. *Centrally located and just off the A14/A12 interchange.*

Shepherd & Dog
Lower Road
Onehouse
Nr. Stowmarket
☎ 01449 612698
Location: (EC P.131)

A charming, C16th pub with beams, an inglenook fireplace and local memorabilia. Tenant, Chris White has already won many prestigious awards due to his various new ideas and he is continuing to make improvements. Greene King ales and a relaxed atmosphere, with regular live entertainment. *1 mile west of the town centre, off the B115.*

Ship Inn
2 Valley Road
Great Clacton

☎ 01255 423324
Location:

This old fashioned pub offers personal service to everyone. Sample delicious, home cooked, traditional fayre like Shepherd's pie and sausage & mash with onions as well as a great value 2 course Sunday lunch for only £5.95. Lovely garden, Sky tv and the pub's not far from the seafront with its own car park. *In the centre of town, at the fork junction.*

Sibton White Horse
Halesworth Road
Sibton

☎ 01728 660337
Location: (EC P.123)

A delightful, C16th free house set in 5 acres of glorious Suffolk countryside, just 20 minutes from Southwold and many other attractions. There are 8 refurbished guest rooms and an excellent revolving menu of fresh and interesting dishes, complemented by superb real ales, wines and single malts. Caravan Club listed. *On the border of Sibton & Peasenhall.*

SIC Szechuan Inn
Cattawade Street
Brantham

☎ 01206 397269
Location: (EC P.132)

This family owned, air conditioned restaurant serves an amazing choice of over 50 dishes including Szechuan, Cantonese and Peking cuisine. Choose from delights like lobster, scallops and Orange duck and there's a takeaway with free delivery service. Outstanding service complements the excellent standard of food. *In the village centre.*

Simla Balti House
26 North Hill
Colchester

☎ 01206 765938/710290
Location: (EC P.128)

This Indian restaurant has such a good reputation that it is frequented by local MP's! You'll find unique dishes such as Balti garlic chilli chicken Mosalla and all dishes are freshly made to order using spices that are ground in the restaurant. Children can eat for half price and there's free delivery within 3 miles. *At the bottom of North Hill.*

20

Spice Zone
1C Head Street
Halstead
☎ 0800 3898698
☎ 01787 479701
Location:

Use the freephone number to experience exquisite Indian food from a menu which features the largest selection of takeaway dishes in Halstead. There are lots of vegetarian options too and a free delivery service within 6 miles if you spend over £10. Open 7 days a week from 5.30-11pm, including Bank Holidays. *Opposite the church.*

Suffolk Punch
429 Norwich Road
Ipswich

☎ 01473 747722
Location: *(EC P.131)*

A very sporty pub which is adorned with flags. Inside there is the hugely popular large screen Sky tv, pool, and darts, with live music on Saturdays and karaoke on Tuesdays; there's always something to do! The best of British bar menu includes a superb all day breakfast, fish & chips and pies. *1 mile northwest of the town centre, on the A1156.*

The Swan Inn (1)
The Street
Little Wadlingfield

☎ 01787 248584
Location:

This traditional, village pub dates to the C15th and has lovely, open fires to relax by. The food is English orientated, with dishes like cottage pie, succulent steaks and jam roly poly. There are 3 well kept real ales to choose from as well as an excellent wine list. 2 en suite guest bedrooms and a nice garden for the summer. *In the centre of the village.*

The Swan Inn (2)
Swan Road
Worlingworth

☎ 01728 628267
Location:

A beautiful, grade II listed building that dates back to the C14th, complete with a thatched roof to give it that idyllic postcard look! Excellent food, utilising fresh, local produce, such as home-made steak & mushroom pie. Children benefit from their own menu and an enclosed garden. Good real ales too. *Centrally located.*

The Tea Rooms
8 High Street
Walton on the Naze

☎ 01255 851119
Location:

This delightful tearoom is just a short walk from the seafront and also sells a wonderful selection of crafts, from wooden toys to local artwork. The menu features toasties, baguettes, soups, salads and an excellent range of teas and coffees. The option to take away is available and you can dine alfresco in summer. *Near both the centre and the seafront.*

**Temptations
Chinese Buffet**
70 Carr Street
Ipswich
☎ 01473 231366
Location:

This new restaurant serves a magnificent range of Oriental dishes from the Pacific Rim. Choose cuisine from countries such as China, Thailand, Malaysia and Japan, and you can dine outside on the large patio in the summer too. Opt for the lunch buffet, or the larger evening buffet, one of the biggest in Ipswich. *Opposite the theatre and cinema.*

21

The Three Ashes Brasserie
Ashes Road
Cressing
☎ 01376 583143
Location: *(EC P.124)*

A lovely, relaxed country pub that has a new brasserie style restaurant. The changing menu utilises local produce to create delicious dishes, from ciabattas and freshly battered cod to roast rump of lamb and calves liver. There's an eclectic wine list too and this is the only pub in Braintree to serve Hoegarden beer! *Just off the A120, south of Braintree.*

Tickle Manor Tearooms
17 High Street
Lavenham

☎ 01787 248438
Location:

This charming tearoom has an open kitchen so you can see and smell the wonderful cooking. Original recipes are used for the delicious array of traditional cakes and you must try the cream teas, oven baked potatoes and superb home-made soups, all with the benefit of waitress service. Enjoy the cosy wood burner too! *In the High Street beside the Avocat shop.*

Trafalgar
616 Main Road
Dovercourt

☎ 01255 502234
Location: *(EC P.117)*

Kevin and Justina have created a lively atmosphere at their C16th pub. A family venue that keeps 2 real ales and serves a range of bar snacks from 12-9pm. There's wide screen tv and a variety of entertainment including live music, theme nights, karaoke, discos and quiz nights - something for everyone! *A mile off the A120 to Harwich, on the B1035.*

Unique
Pallister Road
Clacton on Sea

☎ 01255 225325
Location:

This restaurant is unique in name, style and presentation. Open all day, manager, Diane, serves a glorious selection of English food as well as some interesting Indian dishes. Try the delicious steak & kidney pie and home-made scones, or be tempted by the curries on Fridays and steaks on Saturdays. *Town centre.*

The Vanilla Pod Restaurant
4A Orwell Place
Ipswich
☎ 01473 230254
Location: *(EC P.121)*

Attention to detail is paramount at this beautifully designed restaurant, from the quality of the food to the outstanding service. Experience wonderful dishes like fresh crab, oysters, belly of pork with a Toulouse cassolet and blueberry & white chocolate cheesecake. Extensive wine list and 6 Champagnes. *Opposite St Pancras Catholic Church.*

The Victoria Inn
Felixstowe Ferry
Old Felixstowe

☎ 01394 271636
Location:

A free house set in a beautiful and unique hamlet. Manager Anita Curtis serves 4 real ales including Adnams and IPA and a range of home-made bar food. Try the fish & chips in beer batter and the minted lamb. Lots of nautical memorabilia and lovely views from the non-smoking restaurant of the River Deben and the sea. *3/4 a mile off A14, in the direction of Old Felixstowe.*

The Warwick Arms
121 Pier Avenue
Clacton on Sea

☎ 01255 473656
Location: **(EC P.119)**

Returned to its original name, The Warwick Arms is also under new and improved management. All food is home-made and includes minted lamb shank, freshly battered fish & chips and mouth watering fruit crumbles. Children are catered for, there's a good range of live entertainment and 6 new bedrooms from £25. *Just off the town centre.*

The Water Lily
100 St Helens Street
Ipswich

☎ 01473 257035
Location:

Now under new management, this pub has evolved in to a friendly, good old fashioned drinking venue. All drinks are competitively priced, with cider on tap too, and you can enjoy pool and karaoke every Friday & Sunday. Open all day, the pub has a great atmosphere and there's a nice patio for the summer. *Opposite St Helens Church.*

The Westerfield Railway
Main Road
Westerfield
Nr Ipswich
☎ 01473 252337
Location:

Unsurprisingly close to the station, this welcoming pub serves great beer and good, wholesome food. Choose traditional English pub food or try the diverse range of specials such as Thai green chicken curry or venison served in a red wine sauce. Open all day, this is a perfect venue for all types of function. *Beside the station on the B1077, north of Ipswich.*

White Horse Inn
Edwardstone
Nr Boxford

☎ 01787 211211
Location:

This C16th, former farm house and maltings is now a traditional Suffolk country inn situated in a quiet and tranquil location. 3 real ales are kept and some great old English dishes are served, such as ham, egg & chips and a variety of steamed puddings. Caravaners and campers welcome plus 2 magnificent chalets. *Just off the A1071, east of Sudbury.*

Wig & Fidgett
Straight Road
Boxted

☎ 01206 272227
Location:

This beamed, village pub has a real fire and is now under new management. Malcolm and Louise serve light lunches and an evening bar menu with traditional, home-made dishes such as ham, egg & chips and plus a fine, homely Sunday roast. There are 2 real ales OAP specials on Tuesday and themed evenings. *On the Colchester Road.*

Zentral
Oriental Buffet
25 Head Street
Colchester
☎ 01206 761876
Location:

A venue with an excellent reputation, serving a buffet at both lunch and dinner, where you can eat as much as you like for £12.95. All your favourites, with crispy duck and lamb, spring rolls, satay chicken, spare ribs etc, as well as Chinese and Japanese beers and European wines. Perfect for large parties. *In the centre of Colchester.*

Area 2

Norwich, Wells-Next-The-Sea, Holt, Sheringham, Cromer,
Fakenham, North Walsham, Dereham, Great Yarmouth, Wymondham,
Diss, Beccles, Lowestoft, Southwold
and surrounding areas.

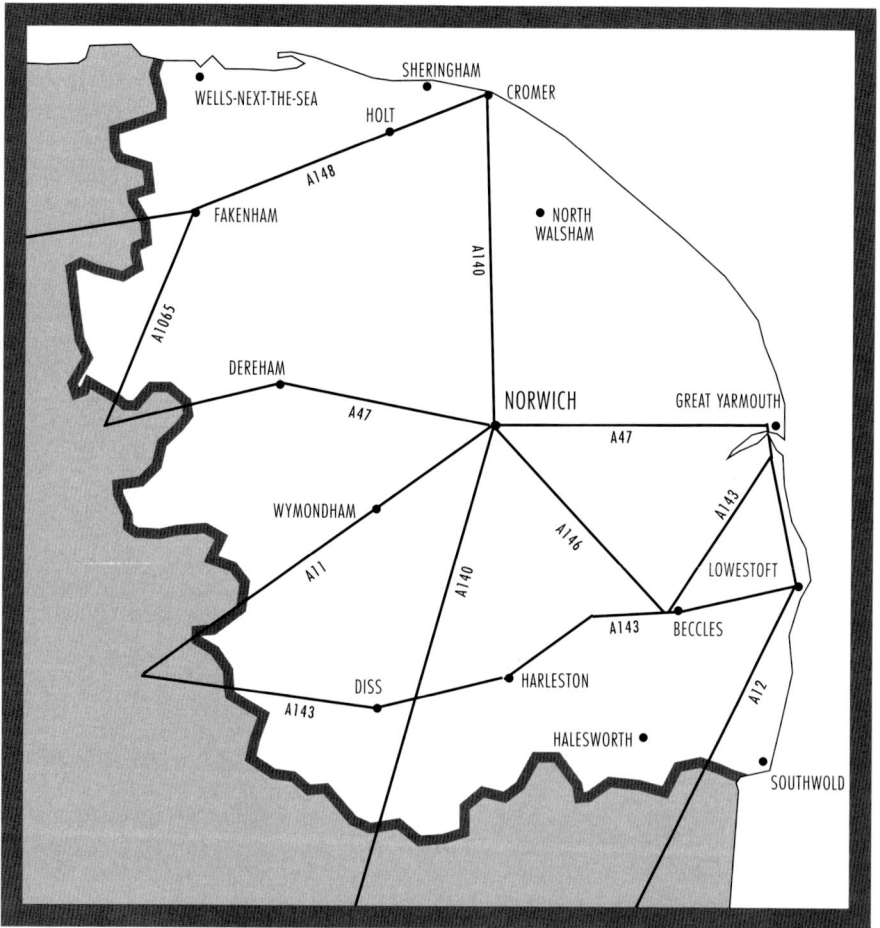

Establishment	Nearest Town	Page No.	Waterside Setting	All Day Opening	Pets Welcome	Takeaway	Real Ales	Rooms From £	No. Bedrooms	Baby Changing	Child Portions	Play Area	Garden	Average Price	No. of Covers	Vegetarian Food	Credit Cards	Functions	Live Music	Coaches Welcome	Air Conditioning	No Smoking	Disabled Access
Ah-So Japanese R.	Norwich	29									•			20	50	•	•	•			•	•	•
Angel Inn	Bungay	29			•	•	2	30	3	•	•		•	6	16	•	•	•	•	•		•	•
Archers E.E.	Great Yarmouth	29			•	•	5				•		•	7.50	100	•	•	•	•	•		•	•
The Avenue	Great Yarmouth	29			•		1				•		•	7	50	•	•	•	•	•		•	•
Bakers Arms	Norwich	29												6	44	•	•	•					•
Barons Court Hotel	Great Yarmouth	29		•				17.50	3		•		•	7.95	30	•	•	•	•	•		•	•
Black Swan (1)	Norwich	30					2	20	14		•		•	6	60	•	•	•				•	•
Black Swan (2)	Swaffham	30				•	3				•		•	3	90	•	•	•	•			•	•
Café Connect	Great Yarmouth	30									•					•	•					•	•
Caxton Arms	Beccles	30					1				•		•			•	•	•					•
Clock Tower H.H	Norwich	30			•		3			•	•		•	6	250	•	•	•	•			•	•
Compleat Angler	Norwich	30				•	5				•		•	5	100	•	•	•	•	•		•	•
The Crawfish Inn	Holt	31				•	2				•		•	7.50	40	•	•	•	•			•	•
The Crown	Norwich	31				•	3						•	5	22	•	•		•			•	•
Crown Fish & Chips	Great Yarmouth	31				•					•			3.50	24	•	•					•	•
Crown Hotel	Watton	31			•		2	25	7		•		•	6.50	70	•	•	•	•	•		•	•
Crown Inn	Diss	31				•	2	27.50	3		•		•	7	60	•	•	•	•			•	•
Duke William	Harleston	31				•	4				•		•	2	30	•	•	•	•			•	•
Duke of York	Bungay	32			•	•	4				•		•	5.75	40	•	•	•	•			•	•
Dukes Head	Holt	32			•	•	3				•		•	6	50	•	•	•	•			•	•
Falcon Inn	Harleston	32				•	2				•		•	5	44	•	•	•	•			•	•
The Ferry House	Norwich	32	•	•	•	•	3				•	•	•	8	54	•	•	•	•	•		•	•
First & Last	Lowestoft	32		•	•	•	2				•		•			•	•	•	•			•	•
Forget Me Not Cafe	Norwich	32									•			6	45	•	•					•	•
George Borrow H.	Lowestoft	33						25	13		•		•	10	7	•	•	•				•	•
George Hotel	Dereham	33			•	•	6	55	8		•			8	100	•	•	•	•	•		•	•
The Globe Inn	Wells Next The Sea	33	•	•	•	•	4	55	7		•		•		80	•	•	•	•			•	•
The Golfers Arms	Great Yarmouth	33		•		•	2				•		•		70	•	•					•	•

25

	Disabled Access	No Smoking	Air Conditioning	Coaches Welcome	Live Music	Functions	Credit Cards	Vegetarian Food	No. of Covers	Average Price	Garden	Play Area	Child Portions	Baby Changing	No. Bedrooms	Rooms From £	Real Ales	Takeaway	Pets Welcome	All Day Opening	Waterside Setting	Page No.	Nearest Town
Great Eastern	•			•	•	•	•	•		1									•			33	Great Yarmouth
The Griffin	•	•		•	•	•	•	•	100	6	•	•	•	•			2	•	•			33	Norwich
Grumpys Cottage R.	•		•				•	•	60	8.50	•		•	•					•			34	Great Yarmouth
Harbour Inn	•			•			•	•	42	5		•	•				3					34	Lowestoft
Hare & Hounds	•				•	•	•	•	40	7.95	•	•	•				2		•		•	34	Holt
Henry IV	•			•		•	•	•	125	6	•		•				3		•			34	Fakenham
Hog in Armour	•					•	•	•	200	7	•		•	•			3	•	•			34	Norwich
Horseshoes	•			•		•	•	•	34	7	•	•	•	•			3		•	•	•	34	Beccles
The Hotel Elizabeth	•			•	•	•	•	•	80	8	•				50	55	2		•		•	35	Great Yarmouth
The Jun-Shon							•	•	120	6									•			35	Norwich
Kings Arms	•					•	•	•	60	3.95	•	•	•	•			13		•		•	35	Norwich
Kings Head Hotel	•			•	•	•	•	•	90	7	•		•	•	8	44	3		•			35	Wroxham
The Lion Inn	•			•	•	•	•	•	100	9	•	•	•	•			3		•	•		35	Great Yarmouth
Lord Nelson (1)	•					•	•	•	24	10	•				4	45	2		•	•		35	Burnham Market
Lord Nelson (2)	•					•	•	•	65	11	•	•					5	•	•	•		36	Burnham Thorpe
Los Locos	•						•	•	70	9								•				36	Lowestoft
Lucky Star C.R.	•						•	•	50	5.50								•	•			36	Lowestoft
Maggie's Cafe							•	•	45	3.90								•	•			36	Gorleston on Sea
The Marine	•			•		•	•	•	60	3.50	•	•	•	•		1			•		•	36	Great Yarmouth
Marley D's Diner	•						•	•	77	5			•									36	Cromer
The Marquee	•				•	•	•	•			•			•			1		•			37	Norwich
Mustard Pot	•					•	•	•	40	6.50	•	•	•	•			5	•	•			37	Dereham
The Norkie	•						•	•	50	5			•					•				37	Norwich
The Old Crown	•				•	•	•	•	34	6.50	•		•			4	4		•			37	Norwich
Old Red House	•						•	•	80		•						2					37	Lowestoft
The Old Workhouse	•				•	•	•	•	30		•		•			4			•			37	Dereham
Ole Frank	•					•	•	•	50	2	•	•	•	•				•	•			38	Lowestoft
Ostrich Inn	•			•		•	•	•	60	7	•	•	•	•	3	30	4		•			38	Fakenham

26

	Disabled Access	No Smoking	Air Conditioning	Coaches Welcome	Live Music	Functions	Credit Cards	Vegetarian Food	No. of Covers	Average Price	Garden	Play Area	Child Portions	Baby Changing	No. Bedrooms	Rooms From £	Real Ales	Takeaway	Pets Welcome	All Day Opening	Waterside Setting	Page No.	Nearest Town
Pizza Express (1)	●	●		●			●	●	125	7			●	●					●			38	Norwich
Pizza Express (2)	●	●	●	●			●	●	200	7.65	●		●	●					●			38	Norwich
The Plough Inn	●			●			●	●	30	8.50	●	●	●		5	3	●	●	●			38	Southwold
Pottergate Tavern	●				●	●	●	●	2							2	●		●	●		38	Norwich
Pyramid Lounge	●			●	●	●	●	●	40	10		●	●						●	●		39	Lowestoft
Quality A.I.R.	●			●		●	●		28				●					●	●			39	Norwich
Railway Tavern	●			●	●	●	●	●	40	4.50	●		●	●		3	●	●	●	●		39	Wroxham
Red Hart Inn	●			●	●	●	●	●	90	7	●		●			3	●		●			39	Holt
Red Lion (1)	●			●		●	●	●	42	6	●		●			3	●		●			39	Wroxham
Red Lion (2)	●			●		●	●	●	200	8	●	●	●			5	●		●		●	39	Wells Next The Sea
The Reef Bar	●			●	●	●	●	●	60	6	●		●			2			●	●	●	40	Stalham
Relish Bar & R.	●			●		●	●	●	50	12			●			2					●	40	Norwich
The R. at Hermanus	●			●	●	●	●	●	320	7.50			●			2				●		40	Great Yarmouth
Robert Kett	●			●	●	●	●	●	72	6.30	●		●	●		4	●		●	●		40	Wymondham
Rosary Tavern	●			●	●	●	●	●	48	3.50	●		●			7	●		●	●		40	Norwich
Royal Oak	●			●	●	●	●	●	40	6.50	●		●			2	●		●	●		40	Halesworth
Sea Breeze	●			●		●	●	●	44	4			●	●				●	●			41	Sheringham
The Ship	●			●	●	●	●	●	30	6	●		●			4	●		●			41	Norwich
Silk Thai Restaurant	●			●		●	●	●	70	9			●					●	●			41	Norwich
Six Bells	●			●	●	●	●	●	40	4	●		●		17	2	●		●			41	Eye
Southlands Hotel	●			●	●	●	●	●	100	10.50	●		●		38.50				●			41	Sheringham
The Steam Packet	●			●		●	●	●					●				●		●			41	Norwich
Sukho Thai	●	●		●			●	●	44	8								●	●			42	Wroxham
Sweet Briar Bistro	●	●		●		●	●	●	34	9			●	●					●			42	Attleborough
Ton Sai	●			●		●	●	●	78	6.50			●					●	●	●		42	Sheringham
The Twin Brothers	●			●		●	●	●	30	7		●	●		3			●	●			42	Dereham
Victoria Inn	●	●		●	●	●	●	●	50	5.50	●	●	●	●	35	4	●		●			42	Wymondham
Village Inn	●	●		●	●	●	●	●	132	8	●	●	●	●		1	●		●	●		42	Norwich

27

	Disabled Access	No Smoking	Air Conditioning	Coaches Welcome	Live Music	Functions	Credit Cards	Vegetarian Food	No. of Covers	Average Price	Garden	Play Area	Child Portions	Baby Changing	No. Bedrooms	Rooms From £	Real Ales	Takeaway	Pets Welcome	All Day Opening	Waterside Setting	Page No.	Nearest Town
The Vine Inn	•	•	•	•	•	•	•	•	32	8	•	•	•		1	60	3	•	•	•		43	Thetford
Welcome	•	•	•	•	•	•											3			•		43	Lowestoft
The Wheatsheaf	•	•		•		•													•			43	Lowestoft
The Wherry Hotel	•	•	•	•	•	•	•	•	70	8	•		•		31	65	2	•	•	•		43	Lowestoft
Wherry Inn	•	•				•	•	•	80	5.95	•		•						•	•		43	Beccles
White Hart	•	•				•	•	•	60	7	•	•	•				5	•	•	•		43	Halesworth
White Horse (1)	•	•				•	•	•	30		•		•				3		•	•		44	Lowestoft
White Horse (2)	•	•				•	•	•	45	7	•		•				5	•	•	•		44	Diss
Windham Arms	•	•				•	•	•	50	7.95	•	•	•				3		•	•		44	Sheringham
Workshop Bar Cafe	•	•	•	•		•	•	•	60	4												44	Norwich
Ye Olde Buck Inn	•	•				•			62	12	•		•				2	•	•	•		44	Dereham
York Tavern	•	•				•	•	•	100	5.95	•	•	•				3		•	•		44	Norwich

28

Ah-So
Japanese Restaurant
16 Prince of Wales Road
Norwich
☎ 01603 618901
Location: (EC P.142)

What a dining experience. Talented chefs cook everything to order, at your table, and juggle knives and eggs too! A full Japanese menu is available, and only the freshest of ingredients are used to create the extensive variety of dishes. The fresh lobster is exquisite as is the selection of vegetarian options. *Near the Anglia Television building. www.ah-so.co.uk*

Angel Inn
Lower Olland Street
Bungay

☎ 01986 892507
Location: (EC P.147)

Dating to 1518, this beamed inn is full of character and has old tunnels leading to the churchyard! Now under new ownership, Tom Burke offers a good selection of traditional English food, with a magnificent Sunday carvery available from 12-4pm at the great value of £5.95. Pretty garden and 3 guest rooms from £30. *At the top end of Mary Street.*

Archers Eating
Emporium
Reedham Ferry Inn
Reedham
☎ 01493 700429
Location: (EC P.150)

David Archer is the proud winner of 'Le Routiers' award for hospitality, first class service and ambience. A riverside free house with its own car ferry, lovely river views, slipway and mooring for 30 boats, as well as a caravan park. A great venue for all the family, with 5 real ales and an international menu. *7 miles south of Acle. Follow signs to Reedham.*

The Avenue
Beatty Road
Great Yarmouth

☎ 01493 842807
Location:

Close to the racecourse, this pub boasts some delightful paintings of amongst others, Desert Orchid, Red Rum and Arkle. Bob and Barbara Bailey serve both a bar and a good quality a la carte menu in the evenings plus a great value Sunday lunch for £4.95. The 40 seater function room opens onto the garden. *Near the racecourse.*

Bakers Arms
66 St Leonards Road
Norwich

☎ 01603 610684
Location:

With ample choice of both draught and bottled beers, this jovial public house is the place to drink and be merry! The B & B rates are excellent value at £17.50 pp, making the Bakers Arms an ideal place to use as a base from which to explore Norwich. Live music every week and small functions are welcomed. *1/2 a mile from the town centre and the riverside.*

Barons Court Hotel
5 Norfolk Square
Great Yarmouth

☎ 01493 843987
Location:

This 14 roomed hotel, with its own car park, is just a 10 minute walk from town and 100 yards from the seafront. An elegant, Edwardian building with good aspects, the rates start from £20 including breakfast, plus an option of a home-made dinner. Newly refurbished, all rooms are en suite and well appointed. *Off the seafront and a short walk from town.*

Black Swan (1)
25 Norwich Road
Horsham St Faith

☎ 01603 897787
Location: *(EC P.136)*

Steeped in history, this friendly village pub has famous former patrons including King Charles II and fighter pilot ace Sir Douglas Bader. Dine in the new, non-smoking restaurant and sample a lovely range of food from home-made curries to a full Sunday roast. Monthly live music and functions are welcomed. *A mile off the A140 and 4 miles north of Norwich.*

Black Swan (2)
The Street
Little Dunham

☎ 01760 722200
Location: *(EC P.148)*

A charming, traditional pub, dating back to the C17th when it was owned by Nelson's uncle, William. Good ales, with Abbot, IPA, and Speckled Hen and a competitive wine list. The food is superb, with lots of fresh fish, including a lovely smoked haddock dish, roast pork, lamb and steaks. Nice garden too. *Close to the museum.*

Cafe Connect
Marina Centre
Marine Parade
Great Yarmouth
☎ 01493 851521
Location:

This fantastic, new restaurant is part of the Marina Centre which boasts a swimming pool, bowls, snooker and a fitness centre. You'll find great value food from fresh baguettes and juicy burgers to crispy salads and wholesome lasagne, with the option to takeaway too. Open all day, non-smoking throughout. *On the seafront.*

Caxton Arms
1 Douglas Place
Ravensmere
Beccles
☎ 01502 714820
Location:

Lovely to find a traditional, family run, drinking only pub. Close to the River Waveney, this free house is open all day with plenty of pub games, Sky tv and free pool and jukebox on Sunday evenings. The guest ale changes each week and you'll appreciate the friendly environment with lots of folk to chat to. *Close to the River Waveney.*

The Clock Tower
Hungry Horse
26 Jarrod Way
Bowthorpe
☎ 01603 748068
Location: *(V P.229)*

This spacious, air conditioned venue boasts its own 150 person function room. The pub opens from 11am so you can drop in and enjoy a coffee, whilst later you can sample a varied menu with favourites like steaks, gourmet burgers or Cod Almighty! Great fun for all the family and kids have their own play areas. *To the west of Norwich.*

Compleat Angler
120 Prince of Wales Road
Norwich

☎ 01603 622425
Location:

This has got the lot. Centrally located, just 600 yards from the cathedral, a riverside frontage and now with a new sheltered river terrace. 5 well kept real ales, wines from around the world and a good selection of traditional pub food like fresh fish & chips and crusty pies. Free function room available for up to 60. *On the edge of the town centre, beside the river.*

30

The Crawfish Inn
Holt Road
Thursford

☎ 01328 878313
Location: **(EC P.140)**

You'll find the best of both here! A traditional bar and a beautifully designed Thai restaurant serving authentic Thai cuisine, freshly prepared using fresh, traditional herbs & spices flown in every week from Thailand, complemented by good wines and Singha beer. *www.realthaifood.co.uk* **On the A148 between Holt & Fakenham.**

The Crown
Ollands Road
Reepham

☎ 01603 870964
Location:

New manager, Stephen Jackson has created a lively atmosphere at this 300 year old pub. He serves 3 real ales and a nice menu that features delicious pizzas, summer barbecues and OAPs can eat 2 courses for just £5. Now open all day, this is a family pub and kids love the play area. Outside bar and catering available. **On the edge of the village.**

Crown Fish & Chips
Restaurant & Takeaway
1 Nelson Road North
Great Yarmouth
☎ 01493 851535
Location:

New owner Okkas Olgar runs this super restaurant with a takeaway facility too. Choose from freshly battered fish like cod, haddock and plaice to more unusual items like rock eel, as well as burgers and sausages. Open from 11am-11pm, this is the place to come to taste fantastic fish & chips, any time of day. **In the centre.**

Crown Hotel
25 High Street
Watton

☎ 01953 882375
Location: **(EC P.141)**

This historic coaching inn has been sympathetically refurbished and is now run by Shirley and Hayley. A lovely, warm atmosphere coupled with friendly service where you can enjoy bar snacks for lunch and an extensive evening menu for dinner. Nice rooms at excellent rates makes this an ideal venue to stay. **On the main road (B1108), through Watton.**

Crown Inn
The Green
Pulham Market

☎ 01379 676652
Location: **(EC P.142)**

Now run by Alister Dwelly, who serves a super menu of delicious, home cooked food such as bangers & mash, cottage pie and a curry of the day. Dating to 1610, the pub has retained many original features and has 2 cosy fires. Next to the church, with an 80 seat private room, it is an ideal venue for functions. **Beside the church.**

Duke William
28 Redenhall Road
Harleston

☎ 01379 853183
Location:

Just a short walk from the town centre, this C17th family owned free house with 4 real ales on tap and many microbrew selections, has been recognised by CAMRA for its high standard of beer. There's a lunchtime bar snack menu, pub games and a pub quiz on Sundays. All day opening and beer garden. **Just off the town centre.**

31

Duke of York
8 Norwich Road
Ditchingham

☎ 01986 895558
Location: (EC P.147)

Now run by Ian & Tina who provide a warm welcome to the whole family. They serve an excellent menu of home cooked, English fayre with wholesome dishes such as Shepherd's pie plus gorgeous, locally produced desserts and ice-creams. Variety of entertainment and organised games nights 4 evenings a week. *Just off the 'Chicken' roundabout on the A143.*

Dukes Head
The Street
Corpusty
Nr. Aylsham
☎ 01263 587529
Location:

A really friendly village pub, with a great atmosphere, opposite the green. Newly refurbished and with a large garden which is splendid in summer, where you can hire a marquee for parties. Michael and Emma offer a warm welcome and serve 3 well kept real ales and a good choice of traditional, home-made pub food. *Off the B1149, in the village centre.*

Falcon Inn
The Green
Pulham Market
Nr Harleston
☎ 01379 676268
Location: (EC P.144)

Michael & Beverley Smith welcome you to their archetypal village local - it's even located on the village green! The new chef produces a fantastic array of fresh dishes like Thai curries and mushroom Stroganoff plus super home-made desserts such as apple pie and Bakewell tart. Family area and fun entertainment. *On the village green.*

The Ferry House
Ferry Road
Surlingham

☎ 01508 538659
Location:

On the banks of the River Yare, this traditional pub dates to 1725. The garden leads down to the river, where there are moorings for boats and delightful views of the river from both the pub and the patio. Good food too, like liver, sausage & bacon casserole, making this an ideal family destination. *On the edge of the village, beside the river.*

First & Last
Dove Street
Lowestoft

☎ 01502 588225
Location:

Everyone is made to feel welcome at this good, old fashioned, friendly drinking pub, open all day from 11.30am until late. Lots to do with pool, darts, live bands every Friday and a Saturday night sing-along. 2 real ales to sample, Greene King IPA and Abbott, plus a full selection of spirits and bottled drinks. *In northern Lowestoft.*

Forget Me Not Cafe
St Michaels at Plea Church
Redwell Street
Norwich
☎ 01603 723411
Location:

Named after the clock, dating from 1857, sited within this C14th deconsecrated church, you'll find a super range of both drinks and food. Try Norfolk apple juice, a choice of coffees and teas and wine and beer too. Delicious snacks and light lunches like broccoli, stilton & pear soup, toasties and lemon drizzle cake. *In the town centre.*

32

George Borrow Hotel
Bridge Road
Oulton Broad
Lowestoft
☎ 01502 569245
Location:

Close to the Broads and the seaside, this is a great location to explore from. 13 bedrooms, including a family room and a honeymoon suite, plus a fantastic range of food from curries and Mexican chicken to fresh fish, steaks and home-made rhubarb crumble. Excellent service and an ideal venue for functions. *Beside the railway crossing in the centre.*

The George Hotel
Swaffham Road
Dereham

☎ 01362 696801
Location: (EC P.139)

This delightful hotel, which dates from the C16th and is grade II listed, has 8 en suite guest rooms which are newly refurbished. High quality food is served on both the bar and a la carte menus with traditional home-made dishes which include succulent steaks and fresh fish. Lovely new conservatory and lounge area. *At the end of the High Street.*

The Globe Inn
The Buttlands
Wells Next The Sea

☎ 01328 710206
Location:

Situated facing a large green and with a secure, suntrap courtyard making it ideal for families. There's a fantastic menu, which changes seasonally and uses the best of Norfolk produce. Try game from the Holkham estate, fresh fish and seafood and locally farmed meat, and you'll be amazed by the service too. *Opposite the green.*

The Golfers Arms
North Denes Road
Great Yarmouth

☎ 01493 843574
Location:

Formerly the 19th hole of a golf course, this lovely free house is celebrating its centenary this year. New landlord, Steven French has introduced large screen Sky tv, to show all the major sports events, as well as a pool competition every Monday. Join in the karaoke Friday to Sunday and there's occasional live music. *Close to the seafront.*

Great Eastern
155 Nelson Road
Great Yarmouth

☎ 01493 331867
Location:

New tenants, Lynette and Paul have refurbished their lively pub to give it a fresh, bright look. There's a good range of drinks with house doubles priced at £1.80! Lots going on with pool, popular karaoke on Fridays and Sundays and live music every Saturday. Open all day and just a short stroll from the seafront. *On the edge of the town centre, close to the sea.*

The Griffin
212 Yarmouth Road
Thorpe St Andrew

☎ 01603 439211
Location:

Completely refurbished, this family run pub and restaurant, with 2 open fires, now has both smoking and non-smoking bars with comfy leather sofas. Good quality, home-made food is served and there are 2 seasonally changing guest ales. Play area, live music & singalongs, barbecues and a marquee for functions. *Off the A47, east of Norwich.*

Grumpys
Cottage Restaurant
Old Road
Acle
☎ 01493 751111
Location:

A friendly restaurant that excels in home cooking, utilising fresh, local produce. Enjoy delights such as slow roasted shoulder of lamb, vegetable crepes and a super selection of locally caught fish. Open lunchtimes and evenings, there's a good choice of reasonably priced wines and a full range of drinks from the bar. *Just off the High Street.*

Harbour Inn &
Faith Nightclub
Royal Plain
Lowestoft
☎ 01502 587408
Location:

One of the most admired daytime and nightime venues in town. Right on the seafront with excellent views from the bar, where you can enjoy a seasonally varied menu, with pensioners specials very popular. The 1st & 2nd floor club is themed on a church, with the DJ in the pulpit playing varied chart numbers! *South side of the bridge, a few miles from the seafront.*

Hare & Hounds
Baconsthorpe Road
Baconsthorpe

☎ 01263 712329
Location:

Now owned by Terry & Val Purkiss who have created a friendly and welcoming atmosphere at their traditional free house, complete with old beams and a real fire. They serve country cooking, like liver & bacon and steak & kidney pudding, and lovely home-made desserts. 4 en suite rooms for letting. *Heading towards Baconsthorpe Castle.*

Henry IV
Greenway Lane
Fakenham

☎ 01328 864592
Location: (V P.229)

Situated just off the town centre, the Henry IV is now part of Greene King's 'Hungry Horse' brand. Manageress Leona Soanes serves a wide range of food from enormous big plate specials to lighter, healthy snacks. A family orientated ambience with Sky Sports, plus a nice beer garden and a small patio with play area. *Just off the A148 and 1 mile from the town centre.*

The Hog in Armour
16 Charing Cross
Norwich

☎ 01603 660355
Location: (EC P.144)

A Master Chef of Great Britain, Kevin Gardner has revitalised this lovely pub, with the emphasis on quality of food and service. He serves a Sunday carvery, with 5 choices of meat plus Asian curries and beautifully prepared dishes from Italy. Live music every Sunday and 2 large function rooms. *Next to Strangers Hall Museum.*

Horseshoes
Cromwell Road
Ringsfield

☎ 01502 713114
Location:

This pleasant, traditional pub has a super selection of home-made food with delights such as steak & kidney pudding, crispy salads, fresh fish and succulent steaks. Beer drinkers will love the choice of real ales and if you're in a hurry, there's an efficient takeaway service. Secure garden and functions are welcomed. *On the edge of the village, off the A145.*

Directory

The Hotel Elizabeth
1 Marine Parade
Great Yarmouth

☎ 01493 855551
Location:

Part of the 'Hotel Elizabeth Group', this well appointed hotel has 50 en suite rooms, including 10 with sea views and 3 luxury suites complete with jacuzzi baths. The menu boasts traditional bar meals like homely sausage & mash and fresh fish & chips and stunning, seasonally changing, a la carte cuisine.
On the Parade, facing the sea.

The Jun-Shon Floating Chinese Restaurant
Riverside
Norwich
☎ 01603 611129
Location: (EC P.148)

This converted junk is a remarkable venue in which to enjoy an extensive Chinese menu, created by experienced chefs, in either the galley or on the top deck (lovely riverside views). High quality, unique dishes are complemented by superb wines and Oriental beers. This is an ideal place for parties and functions.
On the river, beside the railway station.

Kings Arms
22 Hall Road
Norwich

☎ 01603 766361
Location: (EC P.137)

A traditional pub that has historically been voted 'Pub of the Year' by the Norwich Evening News and is listed in the CAMRA Beer Guide. Sample 13 real ales, including 8 guest ales, in a friendly environment with no music and no machines! Good lunchtime bar menu and you can bring in your own takeaway!
1/2 a mile from the town centre. kings-arms@tascali.co.uk

Kings Head Country Carvery & Hotel
Station Road
Hoveton
☎ 01603 782429
Location:

Nice to find a carvery that is available every day of the week, and there's a great offer of 2 meals for £10 from Monday to Saturday. Specials are available too, including vegetarian options, plus a full bar menu, and there's a good choice of wines and real ales. The rooms are superb value as well at only £44 per room.
In the centre of Hoveton.

The Lion Inn
The Street
Thurne

☎ 01692 670796
Location: (EC P.143)

This C17th, grade II listed building was originally an Old Lords House but now has a nautical feel to it and is adorned with local artists' pictures. The menu features home cooking with delights such as locally caught Fisherman's Platter, succulent steaks and magnificent curries. Open fires and a childrens menu at £3.95.
On the Thurne Mouth Dyke.

Lord Nelson (1)
Creake Road
Burnham Market

☎ 01328 738321
Location:

You'll find great food and great beer at this C18th pub, now run by George and Heather. There's a super choice of fresh fish and a range of succulent steaks, as well as delicious desserts like profiteroles and Baileys Creme Brûlée. Awarded a 4 diamond status, there are 4 en suite guest rooms from £45 with breakfast.
Just off the North Norfolk coast road.

35

Lord Nelson (2)
1 Walsingham Road
Burnham Thorpe

☎ 01328 738241
Location: **(EC P.149)**

The lord, born in the village, was a regular in the pub that is now almost a museum to Nelson, with some superb artefacts. An AA Rosette holder, great food with fish, meat, local produce plus good vegetarian dishes. Real ales include Nelson's Revenge from the barrel and Nelson's Blood, a rum based tipple. *In the centre of the village.*

Los Locos Mexican Restaurant & Bar
85-86 High Street
Lowestoft
☎ 01502 561222
Location:

A great, Mexican restaurant serving authentic food such as Fajitas, Burritos and Enchiladas, as well as a special burger menu and an interesting dish called beef and cactus Tangine, made with real cactus! There's a lively bar too, serving traditional Mexican drinks like Sol, Corona, draught San Miguel and Margaritas. *At the bottom of the High Street, on the north side.*

Lucky Star Chinese Restaurant
7-8 Pier Terrace
Lowestoft
☎ 01502 573397
Location: **(EC P.134)**

A fabulous new restaurant that boasts excellent Chinese food and first class service. Owner and chef, Mike Hy, has vast experience of working in London's China Town and offers a traditional Chinese menu and super house specials. Warm and welcoming, with a separate lounge perfect for pre-dinner drinks. *Just over the bridge, on the south side.*

Maggie's Cafe
14-17 Lower
Marine Parade
Gorleston on Sea
☎ 01493 442149
Location:

Open from dawn until dusk, Maggie and Steven have kept the traditional cafe menu but added some fabulous new items. With chicken roast dinner, 5 bean and chilli casserole, cheese & brocolli bake and chocolate lumpy bumpy. Right on the beach with an ice-cream parlour too. Show this guide for a free cuppa! *On the beachfront, close to the town centre.*

The Marine
Marine Parade
Great Yarmouth

☎ 01493 844331
Location: **(EC P.145)**

Sited on the seafront, with nice sea views, this pub is now run by Anne Bishop. Food is served all day, with delights such as home-made Shepherds pie and curries, while kids can have a main course, drink and ice-cream for just £1.95. Lots going on, with live music, Elvis nights and plenty of pub games. *Opposite the jetty on the seafront.*

Marley D's Diner
Oakleigh House
14 Garden Street
Cromer
☎ 01263 513000
Location:

Now under new and improved ownership, Michael and Joanne Clayden serve a lovely, traditional cafe menu from toasties to roast dinners and mouth watering cakes. Indulge in takeaway picnic hampers in the summer or taste one of their delicious ice-creams. Open all day every day, with good disabled facilities. *A few yards from the seafront.*

The Marquee at the Shire Hall
25 Cattle Market Street
Norwich
☎ 01603 440116
Location: (EC P.146)

Adorned with Black Anna memorabilia, the famous jazz singer from the 1930s, this lively music venue features alternative and raw entertainment every night of the week. Something for everyone, with ska, punk, jazz, indie and metal, and a good range of draught lagers and a full selection of bottled drinks. *Opposite the main castle mall entrance.*

The Mustard Pot
Dereham Road
Whinburgh

☎ 01362 692179
Location:

Dating back to 1635, the building was originally 3 separate farm workers' cottages. Now it is a wonderful free house, with 5 real ales including a guest ale, that is commended by CAMRA . Super, home cooked food, with a variety of dishes including grills, fresh fish and a special treat, real hand cut chips! *On the B1135, a mile southeast of Dereham.*

The Norkie
Bowthorpe Main Centre
Bowthorpe

☎ 01603 748851
Location:

This air conditioned, family orientated pub is now under new ownership and features excellent live entertainment every Friday and Sunday night. There's large screen Sky tv too, with the Premiership Plus package, and a good bar menu. The courtyard is ideal for children and is also the venue for summer barbecues. *West of Norwich, in the Bowthorpe Centre.*

The Old Crown
Crown Road
Buxton

☎ 01603 279958
Location:

This C17th inn with an enclosed garden is ideal for families with children, and dogs are welcome too! The chef has created an extensive, home-made English menu, which regularly changes, plus a great Sunday roast served from 12-7pm. OAPs will appreciate their £3.95 lunches from Tuesday to Friday. *2 miles east of the A140 and 7 miles north of Norwich.*

The Old Red House
The Street
Carlton Colville

☎ 01502 561764
Location:

This traditional English pub has blossomed into a lively, village local that welcomes families. There's a delightful patio for the summer, complete with a water feature, large screen Sky tv and popular themed nights. Nice to find a good, drinking only pub for all age groups, with pool and darts teams too! *Opposite the garage.*

The Old Workhouse
The Street
Bawdeswell

☎ 01362 688575
Location:

This small and cosy pub was formerly a workhouse in 1760 and the walls are adorned with old photos and lots of interesting local memorabilia. 4 real ales to sample and plenty of Belgian bottled beers too, plus delicious hot-pots such as Cottage pie, spaghetti Bolognaise, chilli, lamb hotpot and cauliflower cheese. *Centre of the village.*

Ole Frank
Gresham Avenue
Oulton Broad

☎ 01502 562007
Location:

Named after a stuffed heron displayed in a glass cabinet, this family friendly pub, now run by the High family, has been given a new and fresh look. They offer a selection of fresh sandwiches and pies and provide plenty of entertainment with Sky tv, a quiz night every other Sunday, pool, darts and monthly live music. *2 miles west of Lowestoft and a mile from the town centre.*

Ostrich Inn
Fakenham Road
South Creake

☎ 01328 823320
Location: (EC P.153)

This delightful, grade II listed free house is now under new ownership. Try the delicious home-made soup or ciabattas at lunchtime or sample stuffed Mediterranean chicken or skate wings in the evening. You can even dine alfresco in the sunny courtyard. 3 en suite guest rooms from £30 pp with breakfast. *On the B1355 between Fakenham and Burnham Market.*

Pizza Express (1)
15 St Benedict Street
Norwich

☎ 01603 622157
Location:

A really relaxed venue with a contemporary interior and comfy sofas. There is now a brand new menu featuring many of the old favourites as well as some delicious new creations, such as the delicious Pancetta salad. A lovely restaurant where you are assured of quality Italian food as well as a monthly jazz evening! *On the edge of the town centre.*

Pizza Express (2)
The Forum
Millennium Plane
Norwich
☎ 01603 662234
Location:

The Forum is a modern, prestigious building which houses this popular Italian restaurant. Situated on the first floor, the views across the city are amazing. All this, and great food too, from fresh salads to a fantastic choice of pizzas and pasta dishes, complemented by a nice range of Italian wines and bottled beers. *On the first floor of the Forum, in the city centre.*

The Plough Inn
High Street
Wangford

☎ 01502 578239
Location: (EC P.143)

This lovely inn has beautiful landscaped gardens and 5 new, en suite rooms, including 1 disabled room with a private courtyard. The eclectic menu includes super dishes such as Thai market fish in water melon curry and hearty bangers & mash, plus a great range of desserts like creme brûlée and sticky toffee pudding. *On the A12. www.the-plough.biz*

Pottergate Tavern
23 Pottergate
Norwich

☎ 01603 614589
Location:

A traditional, city centre pub, now run by Caragh King who has a relaxed music policy with live music from Wednesday to Sunday. She has also introduced fresh rolls so you can have a bite to eat with a relaxing pint! Enjoy 'fair trade' tea and coffee, organic hot chocolate, traditional pub games and pool. *Near The Market.*

Directory

The Pyramid Lounge
Bar & Restaurant
58 Bridge Road
Oulton Broad
☎ 01502 560005
Location:

This modern style bar and restaurant offers first class food and first class entertainment. Superb cuisine from full English breakfast to modern Fusion style dishes. You can also dine alfresco on the heated patio. Lots going on with DJs, live music and a large screen for music videos and Sky Sports.
In the centre of town and just a short walk from the waterside.

Quality Authentic
Indian Restaurant
100 Harvey Lane
Norwich
☎ 01603 700766
Location: *(EC P.149)*

The chef is a Master Chef award winner for 2003 and they have been commended for their excellence in The Curry Guide. Nice to see an open kitchen so you can enjoy the skills of the chefs preparing this varied Indian cuisine. Free delivery within 5 miles on orders over £15 and 20% off takeaways on Thursdays.
2 miles northeast of the town centre.

Railway Tavern
Station Road
Coltishall

☎ 01603 738316
Location: *(EC P.141)*

This charming, C17th free house is set in 2 acres of grounds and can be described as 'a proper village pub'. It is recognised by CAMRA and keeps 3 real ales, with guests from both major and micro breweries. Under new management, you'll be assured of freshly cooked food. Live bands, karaoke, quiz, pool and Sky tv.
1/2 a mile from the village centre.

Red Hart Inn
The Street
Bodham

☎ 01263 588270
Location: *(EC P.139)*

A C17th inn, steeped in history, that serves a good selection of home-made food, such as warming beef & Guinness cobbler and super indulgent deep fried Mars bars. Fine wines and real ales and there's a newly refurbished function room. Caravanners will love the adjacent site with electric hook up. Families welcome.
3 miles southwest of Sheringham on the A148.

Red Lion (1)
Church Street
Coltishall

☎ 01603 737402
Location: *(EC P.152)*

A C17th, historic pub, just a short walk from the River Bure and now owned by Melanie and Peter Lamb. All families are welcome, the little ones will particularly enjoy the soft play area in the family room. 3 good real ales and excellent pub food, with steak & ale pie, fish & chips, lasagne, curries and fruit crumbles.
7 miles north of Norwich, near crossroads of B1150 and B1354.

Red Lion (2)
44 Wells Road
Stiffkey

☎ 01328 830552
Location:

This C17th pub has delightful views over the River Stiffkey and has open fires with a beautiful conservatory leading to a terraced garden. They serve a high standard of English cuisine, with fish the speciality, and use fresh, local produce wherever possible. Open all day in summer, with families welcome.
On the North Norfolk coast road.

The Reef Bar
Beach Road
Sea Palling

☎ 01692 598177
Location:

This seasonal village pub has a real nautical feel to it and is frequented by jet skiers and watersports enthusiasts. Food is available all day, from both the main menu and specials board, with dishes such as sizzling steaks and wholesome vegetable lasagne. 2 real ales and live entertainment every Saturday night. *On the beach.*

Relish
Restaurant & Bar
Old Street
Newton Flotman
☎ 01508 470548
Location: **(EC P.145)**

A C17th inn, close to the River Tas, with old beams, open fires and contemporary artwork on display. Now run by Rachael & Jeremy Parke, who serve a wonderful selection of food, utilising local organic and free-range produce. You can be assured of a super dining experience and don't miss the great theme nights! *8 miles south of Norwich on the A140.*

The Restaurant
At Hermanus
Hermanus L.C.The Holway
Winterton on Sea
☎ 01493 393607
Location: **(EC P.140)**

A fantastic venue overlooking the cliffs and the sea that is open for breakfast from 9am and closes at 10pm. The new menu has delights like Thai crab cakes and monkfish Thermidore and there are regular barbecues held by the swimming pool. Entertainment every night in the summer and a choice of 3 rooms for functions. *On the edge of the village, overlooking the sea.*

Robert Kett
Lime Tree Avenue
Wymondham

☎ 01953 602957
Location: **(EC P.135)**

Named after it's local hero, the meals at this modern pub are excellent, both in terms of quantity and value for money! The 4 real ales are from local brewer Greene King and complement the delicious country fayre perfectly. Plenty to do for all the family with darts, pool, weekly quiz and monthly live music. *A mile north of the town centre.*

Rosary Tavern
95 Rosary Road
Norwich

☎ 01603 666287
Location:

This CAMRA recognised pub serves a tremendous 7 real ales, including 5 regularly changing guest ales, all from local breweries. Just 2 minutes from the train station, the atmosphere is jovial and traditional pub fayre is served at lunchtimes. Try the great all day breakfast, fresh baguettes or the giant filled Yorkies. *2 minutes from the train station.*

Royal Oak
High Street
Laxfield

☎ 01986 798446
Location: **(EC P.136)**

Now run by Martin and Sharon who have introduced a new menu in their non-smoking restaurant. Home-made options include tasty lasagne and steaming Cottage pie, and OAPs will appreciate the 2 course specials on Wednesday for just £5.50. Enjoy the games room with pool, games machines and a jukebox. *Centrally positioned.*

Sea Breeze
23 High Street
Sheringham

☎ 01263 820282
Location:

100 yards from the seafront, this non-smoking restaurant serves quality, home-made food using fresh, local produce. Try the home-made steak pie or the succulent crab salad. Owner, Craig Neale is continuing the children's menu and takeaway service as well as broadening the menu with daily specials. *Near to both the seafront and town centre.*

The Ship
The Street
South Walsham

☎ 01603 270049
Location: (EC P.134)

Giles and Kim Naylor serve a fabulous choice of traditional English food, such as chicken in a Stilton and white wine sauce and liver & onion casserole. Take advantage of their winter warmer offer, where 2 people can eat 2 courses for just £12.50, and their super curry night on Wednesdays. 4 well kept real ales. *Near the village hall.*

Silk Thai Restaurant
17 Saint Benedicts Street
Norwich

☎ 01603 666223
Location:

An authentic Thai restaurant that serves high calibre cuisine in a beautiful atmosphere. The food is carefully presented and there's a nice range of unique Thai salads to try as well as a host of traditional dishes. Open lunchtime and evening every day, and if you're in a hurry, use the popular takeaway menu. *On the edge of the town and close to the Forum.*

Six Bells
High Street
Gislingham

☎ 01379 783349
Location:

This delightful free house is now under new ownership. Barry & Michelle Corney serve a nice selection of real ales and a good range of bar meals, such as fresh fish & chips and succulent steaks. There's a pretty garden for the summer, a well equipped games room, disco or karaoke at weekends and live music. *On the main road through the village.*

Southlands Hotel
3 South Street
Sheringham

☎ 01263 822679
Location:

This family run hotel, under new ownership, is close to many tourist attractions and just 500 yards from the sea. The food is traditional English with the table d'hote priced at £15. All food is home-made and served in a warm and friendly atmosphere. The 17 bedrooms are competitively priced from £38.50 B&B. *Close to the station.*

The Steam Packet
39 Crown Road
Norwich

☎ 01603 441545
Location: (EC P.146)

This quaint pub is steeped in history, with a former hanging gallery where you could pay your halfpenny and watch the locals being hung! Now a traditional drinking pub, there's a full range of drinks, including local ales from Adnams, and the staff are friendly and efficient. Open all day and functions welcome. *Next to Anglia tv.*

41

Sukho Thai
Riverside Centre
Hoveton
Nr Wroxham
☎ 01603 781133
Location: (EC P.151)

This lovely Thai restaurant is so real that it is like eating in Thailand itself! The authentic menu includes unique dishes such as chilli pork, chicken & beef all complemented by bottled beers from Thailand and Singapore. New owner, Siraprapha Mitchell offers a takeaway menu too. *In the centre of the village. www.sukhothainorwich.co.uk*

The Sweet Briar Bistro
Within Peter Beales Roses
London Road
Attleborough
☎ 01953 450134
Location: (EC P.138)

Set in 3 acres of display gardens, this modern bistro has been awarded a 5 star rating by the Eastern Daily Press. Available all day are tasty snacks and light bites, a traditional roast on Sundays and exquisite dishes from the contemporary a la carte menu from Thursday to Saturday evenings. Fully licensed. *2 miles south of Attleborough.*

Ton Sai
36 High Street
Sheringham

☎ 01263 821365
Location: (EC P.137)

Newly opened, this is the only Thai restaurant in the area. Superb cuisine, made from fresh ingredients, and everything is cooked to order so you are guaranteed delicious food. In fact, everything is Thai, from the decor and the uniforms to the beer and the wine! 1st floor function room, with a bar, for 40 people. *200 yards from the seafront, in the centre.*

The Twin brothers
3 Market Place
Dereham

☎ 01362 691193
Location:

New owners, The Lapa family run this delightful bar and restaurant that specialises in authentic Portuguese cuisine. Open all day, every day, you can pop in for a coffee with friends or relax in elegant surroundings for a romantic dinner in the evening. Good selection of drinks plus Portuguese wines and beers. *On the edge of the Market Place.*

Victoria Inn
Church Road
Deopham

☎ 01953 850783
Location:

In the lovely village of Deopham, you'll find this delightful inn with 3 en suite bedrooms. Fresh, local produce is delivered daily to create delights such as stuffed peppers, chilli, fresh fish and salads. 4 real ales to sample and new owners, Donald and Susan Crichton are putting in a new beer garden and play area. *Close to the church.*

Village Inn
Brewers Fayre
School Lane
Little Melton
☎ 01603 810210
Location:

Great to find a friendly pub and restaurant that has had a hearing hoop installed and has Braille and large print menus available. There's a good selection of traditional British food on offer, with excellent steak nights and a generous serving of Sunday lunch. Efficient service, top range of drinks and a quiz on Wednesdays. *50 yards from Little Melton Primary School.*

The Vine Inn
High Street
Hopton

☎ 01953 681466
Location: *(EC P.138)*

Now under the ownership of Roz and Ronnie who have created a cosy atmosphere in which to sample their well kept real ales! You can enjoy a varied menu in the intimate restaurant, from home-made pies to New Zealand lamb, and the kids will love the adventure playground. Self contained room to let in the barn. *On the High Street.*

Welcome
182 London Road North
Lowestoft

☎ 01502 585500
Location:

A real, traditional free house that offers 5 well kept real ales including 3 regularly changing guest ales. Inside is adorned with nautical photos and model ships and you can enjoy darts, dominoes and regular entertainment with live singers every Friday and a spectacular pianist on Sundays! *On the edge of the town centre.*

The Wheatsheaf
108 High Street
Lowestoft

☎ 01502 573864
Location:

This friendly, family orientated pub dates to the C18th and boasts a large function room, complete with its own bar making it an ideal venue for all types of party. Open every day from 11am-11pm, with a late licence until midnight Thursday to Saturday, there are popular discos every week and monthly entertainment. *On the High Street.*

The Wherry Hotel
Bridge Road
Oulton Broad

☎ 01502 516845
Location:

Part of the 'Elizabeth Hotel Group', the Wherry Hotel has 31 bedrooms which are priced from £65 including a fantastic breakfast. The menu features simple bar snacks and a super carvery plus there are 2 real ales to sample and an extensive wine list. Newly refurbished making this an ideal venue for functions. *On the Broads.*

Wherry Inn
7 The Street
Geldeston

☎ 01508 518371
Location: *(EC P.151)*

A delightful C16th pub that has an atmospheric interior with beams and low ceilings, and a covered courtyard. Sarah & Stephen Driver serve traditional English food, including a lovely home-made steak & ale pie and the kids have their own menu. There is regular live music and theme nights throughout the year. *In the centre of the village.*

White Hart
The Thoroughfare
Halesworth

☎ 01986 873386
Location: *(EC P.152)*

A grade II listed pub, adorned with old photographs, that serves fresh, seasonal food 7 days a week. Choose a simple bar snack or opt for the delicious restaurant menu with delights such as freshly battered fish & chips or steak & kidney pudding. 3 Adnams real ales plus 2 regularly changing guests. Open all day. *Right in the town centre.*

White Horse (1)
The Street
Corton

☎ 01502 730294
Location: *(EC P.153)*

Run by the Brighty family, who keep good real ales, with Adnams and IPA, and serve a fine and varied choice of fresh fish, pies and steaks. Try the classic, fish & chips in beer batter. In summer months they put on mouthwatering barbecues which are both extremely popular and enjoyable.
3 miles north of Lowestoft, a mile off the A12.

White Horse (2)
Hopton Road
Thelnetham

☎ 01379 898298
Location:

A country pub that is full of traditional English pub character, with a superb choice of cuisine from simple pub food to an excellent selection of a la carte dishes. The Sunday carvery is great value at £7.95, available 12-4pm, and OAPs can lunch for £3.95 on weekdays. Private function room for 20 covers.
Off the A1066 from Diss.

Windham Arms
15-17 Wyndham Street
Sheringham

☎ 01263 822609
Location:

Graham Bishop has introduced a fabulous new menu with dishes such as Thai curries and fresh seasonal fish. There's a super Sunday lunch too and kids will appreciate their own menu as well as a childrens room with its own pool table. 6 real ales and regular music from the renowned Sheringham Shantymen.
Near the seafront and the town centre.

The Workshop Bar Cafe
53 Earlham Road
Norwich

☎ 01603 615853
Location:

A new, family run venue for Norwich, with an atmosphere that is relaxing and food that is wholesome, organic and 'fair trade'. From 7.30am - 2pm, feast on cakes, paninis and hot muffins, then from 6pm, dine on an exciting range of Italian and Spanish dishes like tapas, pizzas, pastas, kebabs, salads and no chips!
In the city centre.

Ye Olde Buck Inn
29 The Street
Honingham

☎ 01603 880393
Location: *(EC P.135)*

This old fashioned inn has a wonderful aura, with the site dating back to 1349. Taste simple snacks like ciabattas and home-made soup or sample delicious dishes from the a la carte menu like seafood crumble and bread & butter pudding. Kids have a great menu too and there's a marquee for functions up to 120.
In the centre of the village, 1 mile off the A47.

York Tavern
1 Leicester Street
Norwich

☎ 01603 620918
Location:

A spotless pub that provides good food and excellent service. Families are made very welcome and children enjoy the large beer garden. Open all day, you can enjoy traditional food and a smashing curry and a pint on Wednesdays. Monthly quiz, free pool on Mondays, new jukebox and good student discounts.
In the city centre.

Area 3

Cambridge, Kings Lynn, Swaffham,
Downham Market, Lakenheath, Ely, Mildenhall, Thetford,
Bury St Edmunds, Newmarket, Royston, Saffron Walden
and surrounding areas.

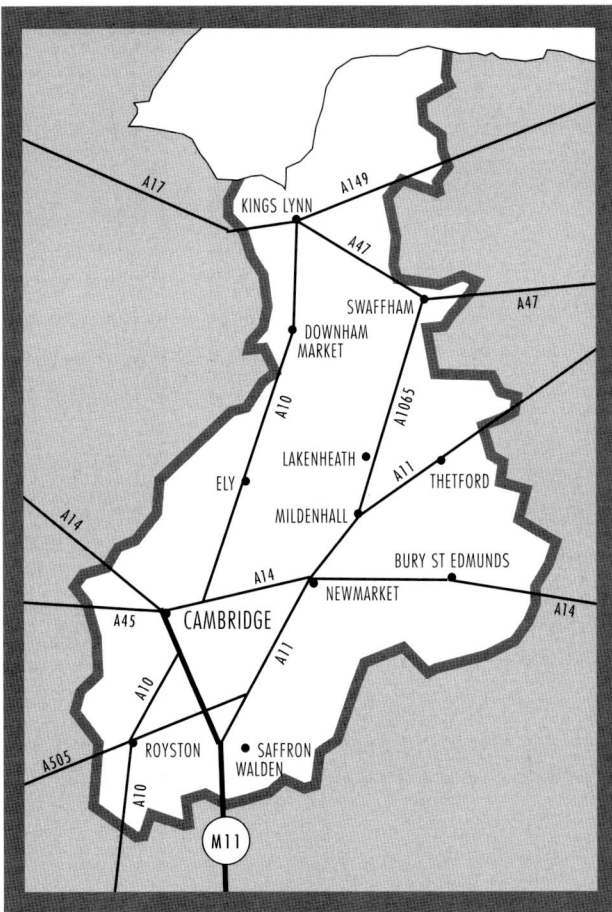

Establishment	Disabled Access	No Smoking	Air Conditioning	Coaches Welcome	Live Music	Functions	Credit Cards	Vegetarian Food	No. of Covers	Average Price	Garden	Play Area	Child Portions	Baby Changing	No. Bedrooms	Rooms from £	Real Ales	Takeaway	Pets Welcome	All Day Opening	Waterside Setting	Page No.	Nearest Town
The Angel	•	•		•	•	•	•	•	100	10	•	•	•				4	•	•	•		51	Kings Lynn
Angels Cafe	•			•			•	•	30	4								•	•	•		51	Mildenhall
Beach Park	•	•	•	•			•	•	60	6.50	•	•	•					•	•	•		51	Hunstanton
Bella Italia	•		•	•		•	•	•	125	6			•				1		•	•		51	Cambridge
Big Buddha	•						•	•	25	7	•	•	•							•	•	51	Cambridge
Black Horse (1)	•			•	•	•	•	•	40	7.50	•		•				4		•			51	Royston
Black Horse (2)	•																					52	Buntingford
Black Horse Inn	•			•		•	•	•	130	6.50	•		•				3		•			52	Kings Lynn
Bottisham Brasserie	•					•	•	•	42	10	•		•									52	Cambridge
Bushel Inn	•			•		•	•	•	60		•		•				2	•	•			52	Newmarket
The Cabinet	•						•										1					52	Royston
Cafe Naz	•			•		•	•	•	60	8									•	•		52	Cambridge
Cafe Rouge	•	•	•	•		•	•	•	125	8.95		•	•						•	•		53	Cambridge
Caffe Uno	•	•	•	•		•	•	•	138	8			•							•		53	Bury St Edmunds
Cat & Fiddle	•			•			•	•	50	5	•		•				3	•	•	•		53	Fakenham
Cazimir	•			•		•	•	•	30											•		53	Cambridge
The Chequers	•	•		•		•	•	•	50	7.95	•		•				2		•	•		53	Brandon
The Chequers Inn	•			•			•	•	30	8	•						3	•	•	•		53	Royston
Cherry Tree	•			•		•	•	•	30	8	•	•	•				3		•	•		54	Ely
Chilis	•			•			•	•	300	9	•	•							•	•		54	Cambridge
The Cock	•			•		•	•	•	50	10	•				3		1	•	•	•		54	Newmarket
The Cock Bar & R.	•	•		•	•	•	•	•	34	9	•		•				3		•	•		54	Sudbury
County Arms	•					•	•	•	30	7	•		•				2		•	•		54	Cambridge
Cromwell Inn	•						•							4	25			•	•	•		54	Lakenheath
Daybreaks								•	22	2.40												55	Ely
Doctor Thirsty's	•	•		•	•	•	•	•	60	5.95									•	•		55	Kings Lynn
Dolphin Inn	•	•		•		•	•	•	64	8	•		•		55	71	3	•	•	•		55	Thetford
Dukes Head Hotel	•	•		•	•	•	•	•	70	12			•				2	•	•	•		55	Kings Lynn

46

	Nearest Town	Page No.	Waterside Setting	All Day Opening	Pets Welcome	Takeaway	Real Ales	Rooms From £	No. Bedrooms	Baby Changing	Child Portions	Play Area	Garden	Average Price	No. of Covers	Vegetarian Food	Credit Cards	Functions	Live Music	Coaches Welcome	Air Conditioning	No Smoking	Disabled Access
Dyke's End	Newmarket	55			•		5				•		•	12	40	•	•	•	•	•		•	•
The Eagle	Kings Lynn	55			•		1				•		•	5	40	•	•	•	•	•			•
Elvedon F. & B.	Thetford	56				•								6	56	•	•	•	•	•		•	•
The Falcon	Bury St Edmunds	56			•	•	3				•	•	•	4.95	90	•	•	•	•	•		•	•
Filipiniana	Lakenheath	56				•								8	35	•	•	•					•
Five Bells	Cambridge	56														•	•					•	•
Five Miles Inn	Soham	56			•		3				•	•		7	100	•	•	•	•	•		•	•
Fleur De Lys	Cambridge	56					3									•	•					•	•
Fox & Hounds	Saffron Walden	57					4					•	•	8	60	•	•	•	•	•		•	•
Gandhi	Cambridge	57				•								10	80	•	•	•					•
The Garden R.	Royston	57									•			6	200	•	•	•	•			•	•
Georgie's R. & B.	Hunstanton	57			•	•	3					•		5.50	50	•	•	•	•	•		•	•
Globe Inn	Mildenhall	57		•	•		3		65				•	5	20	•	•	•	•	•	•	•	•
Golden Ball H. & R.	Cambridge	57			•	•	2	11			•	•	•	12	80	•	•	•	•	•		•	•
Golden Palace	Bury St Edmunds	58			•	•				•		•		9	70	•	•	•					•
Golden Sun T.	Newmarket	58		•	•	•								4.50		•	•	•	•			•	•
The Greengage	Bury St Edmunds	58			•	•	2				•		•	6	100	•	•	•	•	•		•	•
Green Man O&O	Cambridge	58			•	•	2		•		•	•		9	100	•	•	•	•	•		•	•
The Greyhound	Bury St Edmunds	58			•		3				•	•	•	5.95	30	•	•	•	•	•		•	•
Hat & Feathers	Cambridge	58			•		3				•			7	35	•	•	•	•	•		•	•
High Flyer	Ely	59		•	•		2	40	•		•	•	•	7	80	•	•	•	•	•		•	•
The Ickleton Lion	Sawston	59			•		5	6			•			8	50	•	•	•	•	•		•	•
Jolly Brewers	Cambridge	59			•		2	4			•	•	•	7	30	•	•	•	•	•		•	•
King William IV (1)	Royston	59			•		5				•		•	8	80	•	•	•	•	•		•	•
King William IV (2)	March	59					3	3			•			8	60	•	•	•	•	•		•	•
Kings Arms (1)	Bury St Edmunds	59			•	•	5				•			4.25	30	•	•	•	•	•		•	•
Kings Arms (2)	Downham Market	60			•	•	3							6.95	60	•	•	•	•	•		•	•
Kings Head (1)	Newmarket	60			•	•	3					•		6	32	•	•	•	•	•		•	•

47

	Nearest Town	Page No.	Waterside Setting	All Day Opening	Pets Welcome	Takeaway	Real Ales	Rooms From £	No. Bedrooms	Baby Changing	Child Portions	Play Area	Garden	Average Price	No. of Covers	Vegetarian Food	Credit Cards	Functions	Live Music	Coaches Welcome	Air Conditioning	No Smoking	Disabled Access
Kings Head (2)	Cambridge	60			•		4	45	4		•		•	10	64	•	•	•	•	•			•
Kings Head Hotel	Hunstanton	60			•		4	70	9	•	•		•	10	130	•	•	•	•	•			•
The Lifeboat Inn	Hunstanton	60	•		•		8	39	14		•		•	6.50	25	•	•	•	•	•		•	•
Lion & Lamb	Cambridge	60			•		5				•			7.95	30	•	•	•	•	•			•
The Lodge	Brandon	61			•									8	60	•	•	•	•				•
Mai Thai	Cambridge	61			•	•									120	•	•	•					
McDonalds (1)	Bury St Edmunds	61				•				•	•					•	•					•	•
McDonalds (2)	Cambridge	61				•	3				•			3.40	150	•	•					•	•
The Mermaid	Huntingdon	61			•						•		•	8.95	45	•	•	•	•	•			•
Nat. Horseracing	Newmarket	61				•					•			3.25	40	•	•	•					•
Old Coach House	Hunstanton	61			•				10		•			10	50	•	•	•	•	•			•
Old School House	Cambridge	62			•				8		•					•	•	•					•
The Orange House	Newmarket	62			•	•	1	40	6	•	•		•	6	140	•	•	•	•	•			•
The Orange Tree	Hunstanton	62	•		•	•	3		6	•	•		•	8	70	•	•	•	•	•			•
Orchard Tea G'dns	Cambridge	62									•		•	5	140	•	•			•			
Panton Arms	Cambridge	62			•		4				•		•	5.95	70	•	•	•	•	•			
Pemberton Arms	Cambridge	62			•		2				•		•	6	30	•	•	•	•	•			•
Peppercorns	Cambridge	63			•						•	•	•	3.50	10	•	•	•	•	•			•
Pig & Abbot	Royston	63			•		4				•		•	7.50	70	•	•	•	•	•			•
Plough & Fleece	Cambridge	63			•		4				•		•	8	60	•	•	•	•	•			•
Portland Arms	Cambridge	63			•		5				•		•	5	45	•	•	•	•	•			•
Queens Arms	Kings Lynn	63			•		2				•		•	5	30	•	•	•	•	•			•
Queens Head	Cambridge	63			•		3				•			8.50	35	•	•	•	•	•			•
The Red Lion	Thetford	64			•		1				•		•	5	30	•	•	•	•	•			•
Red Lion Inn	Mildenhall	64	•		•		3				•		•	10	80	•	•	•	•	•		•	•
Red Lodge Inn	Mildenhall	64	•		•		3						•	10	80	•	•	•	•	•		•	•
Restaurant 17	Cambridge	64							2					16	60	•	•					•	•
The Rising Sun	Newmarket	64		•			2				•			7.50	40	•	•	•	•	•		•	•

48

Name	Disabled Access	No Smoking	Air Conditioning	Coaches Welcome	Live Music	Functions	Credit Cards	Vegetarian Food	No. of Covers	Average Price	Garden	Play Area	Child Portions	Baby Changing	No. Bedrooms	Rooms From £	Real Ales	Takeaway	Pets Welcome	All Day Opening	Waterside Setting	Page No.	Nearest Town
Riverside Hotel	•	•				•	•	•	50	13	•		•	•		30	2		•	•	•	65	Mildenhall
Romford House		•	•	•		•	•	•	35	11										•		65	Swaffham
Rose of Bengal		•	•	•			•	•	72	10			•					•	•			65	Bury St Edmunds
Royal Bengal							•	•		10												65	Royston
The Royal Oak	•	•				•	•	•	68	6.50	•	•	•				2	•	•	•		65	Bury St Edmunds
The Royal Standard	•					•	•	•	40	5			•				8	•	•	•		65	Cambridge
The Saddle	•					•	•	•	25	6			•				3		•			66	St Neots
Saffron Restaurant	•						•	•	28	9			•									66	Thetford
Sangdao Restaurant							•	•	66	12			•									66	Saffron Walden
Scandinavia C.H.	•	•				•	•	•	56	4	•	•	•					•	•	•		66	Bury St Edmunds
Silk Road II R.		•					•	•	8	7.50			•			35						66	Hunstanton
Silent Wngs	•	•				•	•	•	64	5			•	•	7				•	•		66	St Ives
Silver Spoon C & R	•	•	•		•	•	•	•	56	4			•				3		•	•		67	Kings Lynn
Squirrel's Drey	•					•	•	•	58	10	•	•	•				2		•	•		67	Swaffham
The Swan	•					•	•	•	34	8.50			•				2		•	•		67	Downham Market
The Swan Inn							•	•	20	3												67	Thetford
Tandoori Station	•	•				•	•	•	65	6			•					•	•			67	Cambridge
The Temple Bar	•	•			•	•	•	•	30	6.50	•		•	•	8	30			•	•		67	Newmarket
Thai Light R.							•	•	60	7			•					•	•			68	Halstead
Three Kings Inn	•	•		•		•	•	•	30	10	•	•	•	•	9	57	2		•	•		68	Bury St Edmunds
Tollgate Inn	•	•	•	•		•	•	•	35	5.95	•		•				3		•	•		68	Bury St Edmunds
The Unicorn (1)	•					•	•	•	40	5.95	•		•						•	•		68	Cambridge
The Unicorn (2)	•					•	•	•	70	5.50			•						•	•		68	Cambridge
Waggon & Horses	•					•	•	•	50	5.95	•	•	•				3	•	•	•		68	Newmarket
Wash & Tope Hotel	•	•				•	•	•	70	5.95	•		•	•	10	35	1	•	•	•		69	Hunstanton
Weeping Willow	•					•	•	•	50	8			•				6		•	•		69	Bury St Edmunds
West End	•						•	•	50	6			•				2	•	•	•	•	69	Brandon
White Hart (1)	•					•	•	•	60	3.50	•			•			2	•	•		•	69	Swaffham

49

	Nearest Town	Page No.	Waterside Setting	All Day Opening	Pets Welcome	Takeaway	Real Ales	Rooms From £	No. Bedrooms	Baby Changing	Child Portions	Play Area	Garden	Average Price	No. of Covers	Vegetarian Food	Credit Cards	Functions	Live Music	Coaches Welcome	Air Conditioning	No Smoking	Disabled Access
White Hart (2)	Mildenhall	69			●							●		6	40	●	●	●	●	●	●	●	●
White Hart B. & R.	Cambridge	69			●		3	45	7			●		10	75	●	●	●	●	●	●	●	●
White Horse (1)	Cambridge	70			●		3	50	2			●		9	75	●	●	●	●		●	●	●
White Horse (2)	Cambridge	70			●	●	4				●	●	●	5	55	●	●	●	●	●	●	●	●
White Horse (3)	Cambridge	70			●		2					●	●	10	60	●	●		●		●		●
White Horse (4)	Bury St Edmunds	70				●	3					●		6.50	40	●	●	●		●	●	●	●
White Horse Inn	Brandon	70			●	●	2					●		5	50		●			●	●		●

The Angel
41 School Road
Watlington

☎ 01553 811326
Location: (EC P.172)

Now run by Peter & Mandy, who serve delicious food such as baked trout and Cajun chicken, as well as a roast on Sundays and OAP specials on weekdays. The car park is an ideal venue for summer barbecues, hog roasts and live music plus there are regular discos, bands and theme nights to keep you entertained! *Just off the A10, in the centre of the village.*

Angels Cafe
8 Chiswick Avenue
Mildenhall

☎ 01638 714646
Location:

This high quality cafe has cleanliness which is unsurpassed in the area! Under new ownership and nicely refurbished, there's an extensive array of food such as all day breakfasts, freshly filled baguettes and paninis, a range of fruit and deliciously moist cakes. Friendly, efficient staff and free delivery within 1 mile. *On the industrial estate.*

Beach Park
34 Beach Road
Snettisham

☎ 01485 543763
Location: (EC P.169)

Not far from 'The Wash', you'll find this friendly, family orientated establishment run by Tim & Sandie. They keep a guest real ale and serve a nice variety of food, like lamb shank, salmon in lemon sauce and hot apple pie. There's karaoke twice a week and kids appreciate their own menu with delicious ice-creams! *On the edge of the caravan park.*

Bella Italia
Newnham Mill
Newnham Road
Cambridge
☎ 01223 367507
Location:

Awarded for the quality of their pastas and pizzas, this lovely Italian restaurant also serves a range of steaks and salads. Set in a delightful location, there's a terraced area for the summer months, which overlooks the Mill pond from where you can hire punts. Fabulous water wheel set inside the restaurant. *Close to Fen Causeway, next to the Mill Pond.*

The Big Buddha
Thai Restaurant
67A Bridge Street
Cambridge
☎ 01223 358944
Location: (EC P.163)

Probably the best new restaurant in Cambridge! Fantastic Thai and E-san cuisine, prepared from fresh ingredients flown directly from Thailand, served in a beautifully refurbished environment by staff in traditional Thai costumes. Unique dishes include a lovely spicy duck salad, ant egg curry and deep fried frogs legs. *In the town centre, a short walk from the river.*

Black Horse (1)
63 Orchard Road
Melbourn

☎ 01763 226046
Location: (EC P.171)

Now run by Bryan & Renee Walker, this friendly pub is family orientated with summer barbecues and a kids play area. Superb seasonal menus, highlights being Norfolk steak pie, fresh fish and game, and a super Sunday lunch. Lots going on, with cocktails, wine & cheese as well as live music. *By the business park.*

Black Horse (2)
Brent Pelham
Buntingford

☎ 01279 777305
Location: (EC P.174)

This C16th, former coaching inn boasts great, home-made food on both the bar and a la carte menus, with local produce featuring predominantly. Sunday lunch is superb, served from 1-4pm, and is great value with 2 courses for £11.95. Roaring log fires, a large garden and all types of function are welcomed. *Close to the church.*

Black Horse Inn
Castle Rising
Nr Kings Lynn

☎ 01553 631225
Location: (EC P.154)

This historic C11th inn is located next to a medieval village and just a short walk from the famous castle. Now under the new and enthusiastic ownership of Chris and Julie, this traditional pub serves a wide range of wholesome dishes and children have their own menu. 3 real ales and a delightfully picturesque garden. *Off the A149, centrally located.*

Bottisham Brasserie
4 High Street
Bottisham
Nr Cambridge
☎ 01223 813900
Location: (EC P.161)

Situated in the heart of this picturesque village, this Indian restaurant has a superb menu of authentic dishes, including a large selection of house specialities (try the Tandoori Trout). A friendly atmosphere and efficient service, with Indian beers and 10% off takeaways. Open 7 days a week and fully licensed. *2-3 miles off the A14, between Cambridge and Newmarket.*

Bushel Inn
Market Street
The Rookery
Newmarket
☎ 01638 661727
Location: (EC P.170)

Beautifully refurbished, this comfortable, 500 year old pub has a real sense of history. Excellent food, from homely breakfasts to good, old-fashioned food like mince & mash, stews, home-made soups and a selection of fish and steaks. A wonderful Sunday lunch is served from 3-9pm and fresh produce is guaranteed. *In the centre of The Rookery.*

The Cabinet
High Street
Reed

☎ 01763 848366
Location:

A multi award winning restaurant, including national awards from Remy Martin for best new entrant to the restaurant industry 2006 and an AA rosette. Dating to C16th, the bar has a roaring fire and the restaurant has a contemporary feel with nice furnishings. Incomparable wines and world class service. *In the heart of Reed, 3 miles from Royston.*

Cafe Naz
45-47 Castle Street
Cambridge

☎ 01223 363666
Location:

Voted one of the top 30 restaurants in the U.K. in 2004, Cafe Naz offers a fresh approach to Indian cuisine. The Indian chefs prepare authentic dishes, like Bangladeshi chingri puri and South Indian masalla, which are served in a modern and stylish setting. The function room is ideal for parties and business lunches. *Opposite Shire Hall.*

Directory

Cafe Rouge
25-26 Bridge Street
Cambridge

☎ 01223 364961
Location: (EC P.169)

Beautifully refurbished, this unique brand of restaurant offers something for everyone. Open for breakfast, lunch and dinner, but you can pop in at anytime for a glass of wine or a coffee and relax with the daily papers. All functions welcome and children get a 2 course meal, a drink and an activity pad for only £4.25. *Near Magdalene Bridge.*

Caffe Uno
35 Abbeygate Street
Bury St Edmunds

☎ 01284 756260
Location:

This renowned Italian restaurant encourages customers from all walks of life. The Italian style interior blends sympathetically with the historic C18th building and is a relaxing place to enjoy famous Italian dishes, traditional wines and strong Italian coffee. An ideal venue for any occasion. Kids have their own menu. *Close to Angel Hill and The Abbey.*

Cat & Fiddle
Fakenham Road
East Rudham

☎ 01485 528566
Location: (EC P.158)

Formerly a bakery, this C15th freehouse still retains the old beams and open fires. Now run by Simon and Mary Barker who provide a warm welcome to families. The kids take great delight in having their own menu. Super, traditional dishes plus excellent specials and a Friday steak night. Quiz on Wednesdays. *On the A148 between Fakenham & Kings Lynn.*

Cazimir
13 King Street
Cambridge

☎ 01223 355156
Location: (EC P.185)

This cheerful cafe serves a lovely range of Polish and international light lunches, such as home-made quiches and soups, and an amazing Polish cheesecake. Great drinks too, with a range of coffees, teas, smoothies and soft drinks. Probably one of the best cafes in Cambridge and its open 7 days a week. *In the heart of Cambridge.*

The Chequers
36 Hill Street
Feltwell

☎ 01842 827312
Location: (EC P.166)

New owner, Jackie Sharpe serves outstandingly high quality food. Roast dinners are served 7 days a week and the main menu features tempting dishes such as minted lamb shank, as well as locally sourced fish, steak and game. Well kept real ales and excellent entertainment most weekends. *Next to St Mary's Church.*

The Chequers Inn
London Road
Barley

☎ 01763 848378
Location: (EC P.175)

A charming C17th inn, owned by John and Elizabeth Mann, who serve IPA, Speckled Hen and Ruddles. John is an excellent chef, creating superb dishes like beef & ale pie, braised knuckle of lamb, wild mushroom pasta and game. Join the lunch club and enjoy a 3 course meal for £10.50 and try the Gourmet Evenings. *On the B1368, on the edge of the village.*

53

The Cherry Tree
8 Duck Lane
Haddenham

☎ 01353 740667
Location: **(EC P.160)**

A lovely, country pub serving fine food and well kept real ales. All dishes are freshly prepared, such as delicious home-made pies and tasty curries and there's a pretty garden, home to regular summer barbecues. The ales include Adnams and 2 changing guests plus there's a smashing beer festival every year. *Just behind the High Street, in the village centre.*

Chilis
164-167 Abbeygate Hse.
East Road
Cambridge
☎ 01223 505678
Location:

Voted 'Best Unit' in the UK, an ideal venue for the casual diner. A constantly changing menu of authentic dishes from Mexico and USA, which leaves you spoilt for choice. Large parties can be catered for and booking is advisable at weekends. 'Happy Hour' at the cocktail bar 5-7pm. Familes made most welcome. *Adjacent to the cinema and Grafton shopping centre.*

The Cock
Bury Road
Kentford

☎ 01638 750360
Location:

This 500 year old pub has a sense of history and boasts a large beer garden complete with a peacock! The new menu, prepared by 2 super chefs, features fresh produce and delights such as lambs liver & onions and steak & Guinness pie with mouth watering home-made pastry. Sky tv and 3 new guest rooms. *Between the A11 & A14.*

The Cock Bar
& Restaurant
3 Callis Street
Clare
☎ 01787 277391
Location: **(EC P.159)**

This C15th, Tudor country pub is now run by John and Allyson Rogers. They serve traditional, English food, with international influences, and cater for vegetarians and vegans. An ideal venue for everyone from families to businesses and functions. A super garden, host to summer BBQs & hog roasts. *Close to the castle.*

County Arms
43 Castle Street
Cambridge

☎ 01223 566696
Location:

Now run by award winning chef Kevin Bridges, this homely pub, complete with real fires, offers an eclectic menu. Dishes are named after colleges and schools in Cambridge, with a super steak menu, classic Mexican food and a unique sausage and mash board offering 7 types of sausage and 8 varieties of mash. *Opposite Shire Hall car park.*

Cromwell Inn
76 High Street
Lakenheath

☎ 01842 860308
Location:

The new and friendly landlord, Chris Rickard has big plans for this charming, grade II listed inn which is over 600 years old. The en suite rooms are being updated and prices start from just £25 pp, great value for a town centre pub. Open all day, with a pint from just £2.30 and you can enjoy a game of pool. *In the centre of the High Street.*

Daybreaks
14 Fore Hill
Ely

☎ 01353 666677
Location:

A non-smoking cafe open all day Monday to Saturday from 8.30am-3.30pm. Trevor and Sharon Wilton take pride in using only fresh ingredients to produce a fantastic range of dishes, all prepared to order. Choose from baguettes, pasties, jacket potatoes and locally made cakes. Outside buffets catered for too.
Close to the Market Place.

Doctor Thirsty's
22-24 Norfolk Street
Kings Lynn

☎ 01553 774445
Location:

Mandi Lovegrove and her friendly staff provide a warm and hearty welcome to their modern, yet relaxing pub. Lots of promotions on drinks and a good range of cocktails too, plus a nice selection of food such as all day breakfasts and crusty pies. Really comes to life at the weekend with DJs.
In the centre of Norfolk Street.

Dolphin Inn
Old Market Street
Thetford

☎ 01842 752271
Location: (EC P.168)

Landlady, Gail Coomber serves an extensive menu of home-made food, utilising fresh local produce. Highlights include crusty pies, hot curries, sweet & sour chicken as well as special fish, grill and vegetarian options. Food is available all day on Sundays and there's a pretty beer garden for the summer plus 3 real ales.
On the outskirts of the town centre.

Dukes Head Hotel
Tuesday Market Place
Kings Lynn

☎ 01553 774995
Location:

Dating to 1685, this grade II listed hotel was formerly used for electioneering by Thomas Walpole, Britain's first Prime Minister. Now part of the Elizabeth Hotels Group, there are 71 en suite rooms and 3 function suites making this an ideal venue for business or leisure. Super food and excellent, personal service.
On the Market Place.

The Dyke's End
8 Fair Green
Reach
Nr Cambridge
☎ 01638 743816
Location: (EC P.176)

Owner, Simon Owers, has finished a lovely refurbishment to his fine country pub and now has a new menu focusing on seasonal and locally produced ingredients. Beautifully presented, with generous portions, there's a lunch menu and a choice of evening food, from formal dining to informal bistro bar food.
6 miles west of Newmarket off B1102, beside the village green.

The Eagle
110 Norfolk Street
Kings Lynn

☎ 01553 760447
Location:

New manager, Cheri Day serves high quality, home cooked food at great value prices. Great promotions too, such as 'buy 1 meal, get 1 free' from 5-9pm, plus a Thursday steak night and super curries on Tuesdays. Play pool and darts and enjoy the new entertainment on Sundays with Northern Soul and Motown.
Central Norfolk Street.

Elveden Food Hall
& Bistro
The Courtyard
Elveden
☎ 01842 890790 /01449 612229
Location:

Stacey Gilbert, aka 'The Galloping Chef', creates a wonderful array of freshly made food. He uses local produce and frequents the Farmers Market to produce a varied menu of all the best in British cuisine, including some wonderful pies. A sister venue at the Museum of East Anglian Life in Stowmarket is now open. *Close to the crossroads, opposite the church.*

The Falcon
58 Risbygate Street
Bury St Edmunds

☎ 01284 754128
Location:

One of the oldest pubs in the city, with a friendly and lively atmosphere created by Cynthia & Richard Bidwell. Plenty to do, with pool, darts, Sky tv, floodlit petanque and a quiz every Sunday. Open all day, there are 3 real ales and a good choice of food from fresh baguettes to tuna bake and steaming hot chilli. *On the edge of the town centre.*

Filipiniana
25 High Street
Lakenheath
Nr Brandon
☎ 01842 862660
Location:

A fresh taste for East Anglia, a melting pot of Asia's varied and fascinating cuisines. A real chance to try something different, with exotic dishes like Lumpia, Chicken Adobo and Pancit. The monthly themed Sunday buffet allows you to sample a host of new dishes. Takeaway & delivery service available too. *Between Mildenhall and Brandon, off A1065, near airbase.*

The Five Bells
143-145 High Street
Cherry Hinton
Cambridge
☎ 01223 210787
Location:

New landlord Dave Johnson focuses on entertainment! The pub owns its own race horse, has a 10 pin bowling team, 2 football teams and a golf society! All this, plus an open mike session on Wednesdays, weekend live music, Sky tv, monthly karaoke and a quiz on Sundays. Real ales include Deuchars, IPA and a guest. *On the High Street.*

The Five Miles From
Anywhere No Hurry Inn
Old School Lane
Upware
☎ 01353 721654
Location:

This stunningly attractive inn, with a separate restaurant, has a wonderful choice of fresh, home-made food from the seasonally changing bar and a la carte menus. It's set in large, landscaped grounds in the heart of the Fens and next to the River Cam, with moorings for 25 boats. Expertly managed by Matt and Marissa. *7 miles south of Ely, just off the A1123.*

Fleur De Lys
73 Humberstone Road
Cambridge

☎ 01223 470401
Location:

Well known for being a gay pub, yet everyone is made to feel welcome. Lots going on, with discos every Friday, a top class cabaret and a disco on Saturdays, karaoke every other Sunday and a superb quiz and bingo night on Wednesdays with a free buffet! Open all day, with a full selection of drinks available. *Opposite the Texaco garage.*

Fox & Hounds
High Street
Clavering

☎ 01799 550321
Location:

This historic inn dates from the C13th and is probably the oldest inn in Essex. Beautifully refurbished, you can choose from a delightful menu which includes curries, stir fries and a lovely lamb shank cooked in a minted gravy, plus fresh fish, meats and salads. New takeaway menu and a good wine list too.
On the B1038 in the centre of the village.

The Gandhi
72 Regent Street
Cambridge

☎ 01223 353942
Location: (EC P.162)

A modern Indian restaurant, with authentic surroundings, offering good quality food and extremely efficient service. There is a fine vegetarian selection, as well as house specialities for something different. Discounts of 10% are given to students and on takeaway meals. Booking is recommended at weekends.
Close to Parkers Piece.

The Garden Restaurant
Country Homes & Gdns
Dunsbridge Turnpike
Shepreth
☎ 01763 261543
Location:

This light and airy restaurant is completely non-smoking and is open all day, every day for speciality coffee and a wide range of home-made cakes and an excellent choice of freshly produced snacks, Saturday brunch and traditional Sunday lunch. The daily English breakfast is one of the finest in and around Cambridge.
Beside the A10, close to the village.

Georgie's Restaurant
& Cellar Bar
3 Le Strange Terrace
Hunstanton
☎ 01485 535565
Location:

A fabulous restaurant, open every day in the summer and weekends in the winter, that serves lovely home-made food in a relaxed environment. Choose from delights such as shark, red snapper, steaks and curries, all superbly presented. The warm and friendly bar, open year round, hosts karaoke twice a week.
On the seafront.

Globe Inn
21 Field Road
Mildenhall

☎ 01638 715661
Location:

Jason and Davida Brown now run this friendly pub and serve fresh, home-made food from sandwiches and salads to delicious curries and stews. Awarded a 'Cask Marque' for the quality of their real ales, there's regular live entertainment and summer barbeques held on the new patio area which is secure for kids.
Just off the town centre, on the A1101.

Golden Ball
Hotel & Restaurant
High Street
Boxworth
☎ 01954 267397
Location: (EC P.183)

A delightful, thatched pub, full of character and completely non-smoking. There are 11 well appointed rooms, including a suite and a family room, and a lovely garden with patio heaters. Open for breakfast plus super fresh, home-made food on both the bar and a la carte menus, utilising local produce. Ample car parking.
A mile from the A14.

Golden Palace
Chinese Restaurant
19 Hatter Street
Bury St Edmunds
☎ 01284 754331/704539
Location: (EC P.154)

A superb variety of Oriental cuisine is served here, from Thai curries and Malaysian Satay to a host of Chinese and Cantonese delights. Try the super buffets from Sunday to Thursday evenings where you can 'eat as much as you want' for £14.80, children for £6.50. Takeaway and free local delivery service. *Opposite the cinema.*

Golden Sun Takeaway
94 High Street
Newmarket

☎ 01638 667722
Location:

This fast food venue is under new management and offers an extensive range of food to take-away. There's a new choice of fresh kebabs, like Doner and Sis, and favourites such as juicy burgers and southern fried spicy chicken. Open Monday to Wednesday noon-midnight and Thursday to Sunday 11am-1am. *In the middle of the High Street.*

The Greengage
Hungry Horse
Tollgate Lane
Bury St Edmunds
☎ 01284 760796
Location: (EC P.170)

An excellent venue for the whole family with kids having their own "pick 'n' mix" menu, a play area and a birthday club. Entertainment 6 nights of the week, ranging from bands and karaoke to quizzes and bingo as well as table football, pool, darts, and Sky tv. Wholesome food at great value for money. *On the Eastern outskirts of Bury St Edmunds.*

Green Man
Out & Out
55 High Street
Trumpington
☎ 01223 844903
Location:

A fresh and invigorating interior, combining the best of original features with creative modern design. An original menu, with pastas, fresh fish and meats, often with an interesting twist. Superb value for money, with an excellent 2 course menu for under £8 and good quality and value wines by the glass or bottle. *4 miles south of Cambridge, on the A10.*

The Greyhound
Eastgate Street
Bury St Edmunds

☎ 01284 752358
Location:

Now run by David Wall, this C18th pub has 2 real fires for the winter and a large garden with a bouncy castle for the summer months. David has introduced a new lunchtime menu with steaming jacket potatoes, home-made cottage pie and juicy steaks. Floodlit petanque, pool, Sky tv and a quiz on Mondays. *2 minutes walk from the town centre.*

Hat & Feathers
35 Barton Road
Cambridge

☎ 01223 350723
Location: (EC P.156)

You'll find this traditional pub, that welcomes families, a short walk from the historical city centre of Cambridge. Sean McGuirk serves 3 real ales and has introduced a new menu featuring daily specials and a Sunday roast. Pool competitions on Thursdays, a Sunday quiz, large screen Sky tv and a courtyard with heaters! *Near the junction of Barton Road & Grange Road.*

High Flyer
69 Newnham Street
Ely

☎ 01353 669200
Location:

This is an enchanting, classical building with a sympathetically modernised exterior and an interior of great period charm. The candlelit restaurant serves an international a la carte menu with an extensive wine list, whilst the open plan lounge bar area offers good quality bar food including a choice of 70 sandwiches! *Near the car park on the east side.*

The Ickleton Lion
Abbey Street
Ickleton

☎ 01799 530269
Location: (EC P.173)

New manager and chef, Chris Collinson serves an old-fashioned, traditional English menu, with a changing specials board. Try ham & figs to start with, then calves liver & bacon, finished off with mouth watering, home-made desserts like bread & butter pudding. 5 well kept real ales and a new and extensive wine list. *The only pub in the village!*

The Jolly Brewers
5 Fen Road
Milton
☎ 01223 860585
Location: (EC P.157)

There is a large menu with a great variety and you'll find generous meals of excellent quality and at reasonable prices too. The wines and ales complement the food admirably and the pretty garden is a delight in summer. 4 new en suite rooms. *Just off the main sreet, on the way to the river.*

King William IV (1)
Chishill Road
Heydon
Nr Royston
☎ 01763 838773
Location: (EC P.175)

This C17th free house has won numerous awards, including the 'Bookers Best Pub In UK 2000'. A host of vegetarian dishes plus plenty of choice for meat eaters, including a rich chicken casserole with paprika dumplings. 5 real ales and a nice variety of Old and New World wines. Very high standards in all areas. *2 miles from the A505, on the main road through Heydon.*

King William IV (2)
High Street
March

☎ 01354 653378
Location: (EC P.186)

Newly refurbished and now offering 3 en suite guest bedrooms. A lovely menu, featuring a large range of succulent steaks and wholesome pies, plus delights such as salmon & crab cakes and Mediterranean pasta dishes. 3 well kept real ales and Saturday night entertainment such as karaoke, live music and discos. *1/2 mile from the centre in the High Street.*

Kings Arms (1)
23 Brentgovel Street
Bury St Edmunds

☎ 01284 761874
Location:

Now run by Roger & Nicola Arbon who guarantee a warm atmosphere at their friendly pub. Good food is served from 12-3pm such as filled baguettes and sausage & mash and the portion size and presentation is admirable. Pop in for a coffee with the daily papers or happy hour on weekdays from 5-7pm. *In the centre of town.*

Kings Arms (2)
The Green
Shouldham

☎ 01366 347819
Location: (EC P.184)

'Quite simply unique' - the house motto that truly reflects every aspect of this unusual C17th Norfolk Inn. The setting, style, decor and wonderfully relaxing ambience are all equally complemented by the attentive hospitality and the superb food, prepared from local produce. The sponge puddings are a must!
Opposite The Green and the primary school.

Kings Head (1)
Bridge Street
Moulton

☎ 01638 750156
Location:

This comfortable, village local is now run by Denise Alexander who has created a warm, friendly and informal atmosphere. A true country pub with a nice selection of real ales, petanque, pool, crib and a quiz. Denise serves a lovely, varied menu with delights like mushroom en croute and a delicious pasta bake.
Opposite the village green.

Kings Head (2)
19 High Street
Sawston

☎ 01223 833541
Location:

A traditional alehouse, grade II listed and dating back to the C17th, with a wood burning stove. Landlady, Kay Wheeler-Page offers a good range of real ales, with up to 3 changing guests, a large garden with an enclosure for rabbits, and 4 en suite guest bedrooms from £45 including a nice Continental breakfast.
On the High Street.

Kings Head Hotel
Great Bircham

☎ 01485 578265
Location:

Completely refurbished, this outstanding hotel now has 9 en suite, contemporary rooms complete with tvs and playstations! Super food from a juicy burger with hand-cut chips, seabass in a tomato and vanilla sauce to plum & cinnamon crumble. 4 real ales to sample and an extensive choice of wines and champagnes.
Centrally positioned.

The Lifeboat Inn
Ship Lane
Thornham

☎ 01485 512236
Location: (EC P.182)

This C16th, smugglers ale house is set in one of the most picturesque parts of Norfolk and boasts sea views over the harbour. 8 real ales to sample and delicious, home-made country fayre such as fish pie and mussels cooked in a secret recipe! 14 en suite rooms, a walled garden and a childrens playground.
In the middle of Thornham.

Lion & Lamb
High Street
Milton

☎ 01223 860202
Location:

Landlady Jackie Short runs this friendly village pub close to the historic city of Cambridge. She serves a wonderful selection of 5 real ales, including Artois Boc which is only available in 200 pubs countrywide. Good home cooking and a superb Sunday roast for £7.50 plus excellent entertainment twice a month.
In the centre of the High Street.

The Lodge
29 High Street
Feltwell

☎ 01842 828474
Location: (EC P.165)

A C17th pub and restaurant, now under the ownership of Janet Jackson. She has created a friendly environment and specialises in Mexican food, with delights such as Enchiladas, Tacos and a super Mexican breakfast that includes Chorizo, scrambled eggs and waffles. San Miguel lager too plus an improved wine list. *In the main street of the village.*

Mai Thai
at Hobbs Pavilion
Parker's Piece
Cambridge
☎ 01223 367480
Location: (EC P.159)

This former cricket pavilion is set in a beautiful spot where you can gaze over the famous park and in summer watch a game of cricket or sit and daydream. Host to a contemporary restaurant serving an authentic Thai menu, including a range of light snacks and exciting salads. Ideal for parties and corporate functions. *Beside the University Arms Hotel on Parker's Piece.*

McDonalds (1)
42 Cornhill
Bury St Edmunds

☎ 01284 750569
Location: (EC P.168)

This popular, family orientated restaurant has recently been refurbished with comfortable seating and a fresh decor. Matching the new makeover is an improved menu of healthy options like bagels and salads as well as the McDonalds classics such as juicy burgers and McMuffins. Open 7 days, 6.30am till late. *Outside Cornhill Walk.*

McDonalds (2)
9 Rose Crescent
Cambridge

☎ 01223 303020
Location: (EC P.173)

A modern and clean, family restaurant that is open 7 days a week from 6.30am-11pm and until midnight on Fridays and Saturdays. New items on the menu include Caesar salad, deli sandwiches and fruit bags and children appreciate the colouring pads and balloons, all complemented by friendly service. *Just off the Market Square.*

The Mermaid
High Street
Ellington

☎ 01480 891450
Location:

Step back in time! Discover a truly traditional village pub that dates back to the C14th, with low beams and crooked doorways. Experience superb home cooked food with wholesome dishes such as pheasant pot roast, steak mushroom & ale pie as well as home-made fruit crumbles. *Next to the church.*

National Horseracing
Museum Café
99 High Street
Newmarket
☎ 01638 667333
Location:

Situated in the Museum, the café boasts unique murals of famous racing personalities, many of which have been autographed. Enjoy home cooked meals with a glass of wine, morning coffee or perhaps afternoon tea and in summer relax in the outdoor seating area under the roses. Full access. *In the middle of the High Street.*

The Old Coach House
Pizza Restaurant & Bar
High Street
Thornham
☎ 01485 512236
Location: (EC P.182)

Feel like you are in the Mediterranean! Relax in the calming atmosphere, with nice views of the harbour, and taste superb, home-made food and excellent wines. Choose any combination of toppings for your pizzas or enjoy fresh pasta dishes and crispy salads. 10 top quality en suite bedrooms from £29.
In the middle of Thornham.

The Old School
Guest House
9 Greenside
Waterbeach
☎ 01223 861609
Location: (EC P.185)

A beautifully renovated C18th schoolhouse, which now houses 8 well appointed, en suite bedrooms, from £70, including full English breakfast. A superb base, in this pretty village, for all visitors to nearby Cambridge, with good pubs nearby. A beautiful conservatory lounge and a garden too. Cots available.
Opposite the village green.

The Orange House
146 High Street
Newmarket

☎ 01638 561282
Location:

This large, open plan pub has large screen Sky tv, showing both sport and music videos, as well as pub games including a pool table. Good, wholesome food like sausage & mash with an onion gravy and jumbo fish & chips. You must try the steak nights on Tuesdays and Thursdays where you buy one and get one free!
At the top of the High Street.

The Orange Tree
High Street
Thornham

☎ 01485 512213
Location: (EC P.164)

A family welcoming, C16th inn, in a superb location from which to explore the North Norfolk coast. Terrific food, freshly cooked using local produce, with fish featuring highly on the menu. Sunday lunch is served from 12-6pm and there's a large garden with a play area and 6 en suite rooms including a family room.
5 miles east of Hunstanton on the A149.

Orchard Tea Gardens
45 Millway
Grantchester

☎ 01223 845788
Location: (EC P.184)

The ideal way to finish a gentle punt along the River Cam. Here you can enjoy that most traditional of English virtues; a cream tea with scones and jam in a beautiful orchard in the historic surroundings of Grantchester. Open all year, choose from snacks, light lunches and hot meals. A Shakespeare play venue too.
3 miles south of Cambridge.

Panton Arms
43 Panton Street
Cambridge

☎ 01223 464351
Location:

A traditional pub in the back streets of Cambridge. All the food is home cooked and can be enjoyed in the attractive courtyard in the summer. Try delicious soups, ciabattas, salads, freshly battered fish & chips and a mouth watering steak & mushroom pie. 4 cask ales and an excellent choice of international wines.
Close to the centre, off Lensfield Road.

Pemberton Arms
2 High Street
Harston

☎ 01223 870351
Location: *(EC P.167)*

Tenants Mark & Vickie have made sweeping changes and re-established this into a very popular local venue. Good pub food created by Vickie, ales from Greene King, pub games including pool and darts, as well as a giant screen for sporting events. The new decking area and garden attracts many families. *On the A10 London Road beside the war memorial.*

Peppercorns
3 Rose Crescent
Cambridge

☎ 01223 518863
Location:

Under new ownership, you'll find an innovative array of food from breakfast rolls, wraps and paninis to noodles with duck and hoisin sauce, fresh pasta dishes and crunchy salads. Organic products, high quality cakes and juicy fruit salads make this an enjoyable eating experience! Try Peppercorns Kings Parade too. *Close to the Market Place.*

Pig & Abbot
Abbington Piggots
Nr Royston

☎ 01763 853515
Location: *(EC P.177)*

Nicola Grundy and Pat Thompson have beautifully restored this old English pub/restaurant and have retained all its original features. The 4 well kept real ales include 2 guests which are regularly changed and there are several delicious menus to choose from. Excellent theme evenings and a lovely garden. *In the centre of the village, which is west of Royston.*

Plough & Fleece
High Street
Horningsea

☎ 01223 860795
Location:

Now run by Rachel and Phil, this C16th beamed pub has 2 real fires and a cosy atmosphere. High quality, home-made English food is served with delights such as Romany rabbit, made from a 20 year old recipe, and lots of vegetarian options. 4 well kept real ales, a broad wine list, a large garden and parking. *Opposite the garden centre.*

Portland Arms
129 Chesterton Road
Cambridge

☎ 01223 357268
Location:

A large, city pub, a short walk from the centre of Cambridge with a non-smoking bar and a new beer garden. Renowned as a music venue, there are bands up to 6 nights a week with a good variety of music. CAMRA commended with 5 fine real ales and a nice choice of traditional pub food, with a super Sunday roast. *On Mitcham's Corner.*

Queens Arms
15 London Road
Kings Lynn

☎ 01553 761754
Location:

A lovely pub for traditional home cooked meals from steaks and curries to sweet & sour chicken dishes. Lots to do, with pool, darts and regular live entertainment, karaoke and discos. Salsa dancing or rock 'n' roll on a Tuesday and a skittle alley Sundays, Mondays and Thursdays. Large function room with its own bar. *1/2 a mile from the town centre on the ring road.*

Queens Head
48 Royston Road
Harston

☎ 01223 870693
Location:. (EC P.174)

A lovely, 200 year old village pub serving traditional English fayre that is all freshly prepared and cooked to order. Try the delicious steak & ale pie or the superb Sunday lunch followed by a leisurely game of petanque! There are 3 well kept real ales to try and the enclosed garden makes it ideal for children.
On the A10 on the Royston side of the village.

The Red Lion
Market Place
Thetford

☎ 01842 762966
Location:

In the centre of Thetford, you'll find this grade II listed pub, newly decorated, serving a wide selection of Portuguese food. Open all day, you can choose delicious chicken Piri Piri, fresh fish and spicy sausages as well as Portuguese beer, traditional ale and a range of international wines. Car parking available.
On the Market Place.

Red Lion Inn
The Street
Icklingham

☎ 01638 717802
Location:

By the River Lark, this historic C16th inn and restaurant has retained many period features. Managed by the same team for 15 years, who serve a fine menu using local produce, featuring game, lots of fish dishes as well as delicious home-made sweets. Sited in 2 acres of grounds, with a comfortable lounge bar.
In the centre of the village on the A1101.

The Red Lodge Inn
Turnpike Road
Red Lodge

☎ 01638 750531
Location: (EC P.158)

A lovely C13th, grade II listed building with low beams, plenty of character and a warm and bubbly atmosphere. Good real ales and a wide choice of food like rustic bread with mushrooms and garlic, minted lamb chops and a great value 'Truckers Special' at £6.50, with a pint! Open all day and functions are welcomed.
Close to the Karting Centre.

Restaurant 17
17 Regent Street
Cambridge

☎ 01223 273007
Location:

Linked to De Vere University Arms Hotel, this fabulous city centre restaurant has a menu of traditional, seasonally changing dishes with a modern twist. Featuring game, fish and plenty of vegetarian options, there's something for everyone! Open for lunch and dinner every day with a smashing Sunday roast.
Close to Parkers Piece..

The Rising Sun
11 Sun Street
Isleham

☎ 01638 780471
Location:

Formerly 3 cottages, this grade II listed free house dates to 1605 and now boasts a traditional menu of fresh dishes, with delights such as succulent steaks served with hand cut chips, delicious curries and stuffed aubergines. A beautifully designed garden and 2 en suite guest rooms, with cooking facilities, from Spring.
Next door to the post office.

Directory

Riverside Hotel
Mill Street
Mildenhall

☎ 01638 717274
Location: (EC IFC)

Set by the River Lark, this is one of the leading 3 star hotels in East Anglia. The Riverside has won many industry awards and has retained much of the splendid historic, C18th character to the building. 30 en suite rooms, one with fourposter, and fine a la carte and table d'hote menus as well as simpler snacks. *3 miles from A11, a few minutes walk from the Market Place.*

Romford House
5 London Street
Swaffham

☎ 01760 722552
Location:

A beautiful restaurant, set in a 400 year old building, now owned by Paul & Denise Clayton, who serve an array of Continental bistro style cuisine. This is an ideal venue to enjoy delicious food in charming surroundings, where you can relax near the fire and soak up the atmosphere. Extensive international wine list. *Just off the Market Square.*

Rose of Bengal
Indian Restaurant
109 Risbygate Street
Bury St Edmunds
☎ 01284 717000/700123
Location: (EC P.155)

One of the newest restaurants in this historic city, offering a fine choice of authentic Indian cuisine in a modern atmosphere. Try the delicious house specialities as well as the popular, traditional dishes and you must sample the Indian ice-cream. Open lunch and evening, 7 days a week, with a 10% discount on takeaways. *On the edge of the town centre.*

The Royal Bengal
Tandoori Restaurant
55 High Street
Royston
☎ 01763 241471/236136
Location: (EC P.180)

With over 20 years of experience running Viceroy of India in Buntingford, the owners new outlet serves adventurous, Indian and Bangladeshi dishes of the highest quality. Open 7 days a week, fully licensed and air conditioned, there's a fine choice of creative vegetarian dishes, chef specials and good Indian beers. *At the end of the High Street.*

The Royal Oak
Ixworth Thorpe

☎ 01359 269740
Location: (EC P.172)

Now under permanent management, this traditional, country pub is open for food 7 days a week. Choose from an extensive menu of home-made dishes, including some exciting specials, such as peppered pork casserole, and 2 people can eat for just £8 at lunch time. Nice garden and an amazing kids play area. *On the A1088 in the village centre.*

The Royal Standard
292 Mill Road
Cambridge

☎ 01223 517206
Location:

Now enthusiastically run by John & Wendy who have vastly improved this traditional pub. They serve Greene King IPA and Shepherd Neame Spitfire, plus lots of well kept guest ales, as well as a new menu of home cooked food with daily specials. Monday quiz, Sky tv, entertainment and offers for students. *At the Sainsburys end of Mill Road.*

The Saddle
26 High Street
Kimbolton

☎ 01480 860408
Location:

This clean and bright, country pub has a contemporary restaurant and a delightful garden with patio heaters. Ideal for the whole family, tasty food is served at weekends such as bangers & mash and steak & ale pie. A full range of drinks, including 2 real ales, and excellent entertainment twice a month. *In the centre of the High Street.*

The Saffron Restaurant
17 St Giles Lane
Thetford

☎ 01842 762000/766142
Location:

Good food, good service and a cosy, traditional Indian interior, as well as an award winning, experienced chef make the Saffron a popular venue. Open from 5pm, with late closing at weekends. Sample high quality food from India, Bangladesh & Pakistan, made from fresh ingredients. Free delivery within 3 miles. *Just off the town centre. www.saffron-thetford.com.*

Sangdao Restaurant
14-16 Hill Street
Saffron Walden

☎ 01799 506016
Location: **(EC P.178)**

A real success story, this is the second restaurant, with a third opening in Yorkshire. The secret is authenticity. All spices and sauces are imported and produce the true Thai taste. As well as a Thai interior, you can sample Singa beer, Mekong whiskey and Sangsum Thai rum. It does not get more real than this! *Close to the centre.*

Scandinavia Coffee House
30 Abbeygate Street
Bury St Edmunds
☎ 01284 700853
Location: **(EC P.179)**

Ideally located in the historical part of the town centre, this light and airy coffee house serves a superb and varied selection of fresh sandwiches, hot snacks and mouthwatering home-made cakes. There's a choice of teas and coffees and you must try the speciality chocolate drink. Alfresco dining available too. *At the bottom of Abbeygate Street, opposite the abbey.*

Silk Road II Restaurant
Lavender Hill Services
Lynn Road
Heacham
☎ 01485 572268
Location:

Following the success of Silk Road I in Kings Lynn, Louise Ho has opened her second restaurant in the village of Heacham. The head chef has created one of the best Oriental menus in the area with an unsurpassable aromatic duck. Completely non-smoking, open lunch and evening every day with a takeaway menu too. *A mile south of Hunstanton, on the A149.*

Silent Wings
The Raptor Foundation
St Ives Road
Woodhurst
☎ 01487 741140
Location:

An interesting restaurant where you can browse the displays of birds of prey whilst enjoying something from the tasty menu of delicious dishes. Watch magnificent displays by Liz McQuillen with her owls, falcons, hawks & eagles or wander through the amazing gift and craft shop. Stay over in a lovely en suite room. *Just outside the village on the B1040.*

Directory

Silver Spoon
Cafe & Restaurant
122 Norfolk Street
Kings Lynn
☎ 01553 760057
Location:

Now under new ownership, this bright, cheerful cafe is now open 8am-7pm every day. The cuisine is classically English with a 150 item menu offering everything from full English breakfast to every type of roast. Excellent coffees, as well as herbal & fruit teas, smoothies, milkshakes and a fine range of soft drinks. *Near the main shopping area.*

Squirrel's Drey
70 The Street
Sporle

☎ 01760 724842
Location:

New owners, Barry & Bernadette Allen produce a super array of food in a relaxed country setting. Feast on delicious home-made cooking, such as lamb shank in a red wine jus and a lovely selection of pies. A nice venue with beer garden and an open fire - an ideal place to stop at on the way back from the coast. *Just off the A47, in the centre of the village.*

The Swan
High Street
Fincham

☎ 01366 347765
Location:

A change of ownership and a change of cuisine too! This lovely free house dates to the C17th and the real fires make it a great place to venture to for a quiet drink or a delicious meal. Choose from a 100 item Thai menu, with fantastic noodle dishes, stir fries and curries, to classic English dishes like local ham & eggs. *Off the A1122, in the centre of the village.*

The Swan Inn
Thetford Road
Coney Weston

☎ 01359 221295
Location: (EC P.165)

Now run by Kevin & Jean Collins, this warm and cosy pub is adorned with old photographs connected with USAF Knettishall and research on the penny whistle. They welcome the whole family and serve a good range of bar snacks and Greene King ales. Monthly pub quiz and regular folk jamming sessions. *On the main road and the only pub in the village.*

Tandoori Station
59 Hills Road
Cambridge

☎ 01223 369696
Location: (EC P.157)

Make a stop at the Tandoori Station, a new Indian restaurant that offers a unique concept to Cambridge - an open buffet counter. Dine in style, with 2 courses for just £4.95, from a high quality menu featuring 7 chef's specials. Modern and minimalist in style, open every day with a 10% discount on takeaways. *Not far from the railway station.*

The Temple Bar
Sun Lane
Newmarket

☎ 01638 561661
Location:

The only traditional, Irish pub in Newmarket! You'll find a great atmosphere, where everyone is made to feel welcome, with live music every Friday, from Irish bands to classic folk, rock and karaoke on Sundays. There are now 8 new guest bedrooms from just £30 per person including a full English breakfast. *Just off the High Street.*

67

**Thai Light
Restaurant**
33 High Street
Halstead
☎ 01787 477577
Location: (EC P.179)

A C17th English classical building with a contrasting Thai interior! The award winning chefs provide a diverse range of food, complemented by Thai beers and European wines. You must try the curries and also Weeping Tiger Beef, Pat Thai noodles and duck in plum sauce. Takeaway service available. *In the middle of the High Street.*

Three Kings Inn
The Kings Lodge
Hengrave Road
Fornham All Saints
☎ 01284 766979
Location: (EC P.160)

This old coaching house is now run by Stuart and Karen who have created a friendly and jovial atmosphere. They serve a nice range of traditional English food, with a selection of specials, utilising fresh, locally sourced produce. There are 9 en suite rooms, all well equipped with prices starting from just £57.50. *On the A1101 in the centre of the village.*

Tollgate Inn
142 Fornham Road
Bury St Edmunds

☎ 01284 755237
Location:

A traditional pub, with old beams and real fires, serving an evening a la carte menu and good lunches, all freshly cooked. The succulent steaks are not to be missed and the home-made desserts like Apple Strudel are just superb! A huge garden, with football nets, keeps the kids happy and there are 3 ales too. *A mile east of the town centre.*

The Unicorn (1)
15 High Street
Cherry Hinton

☎ 01223 245872
Location: (EC P.177)

A friendly pub where you can enjoy an excellent range of drinks and superb live entertainment. Something for everyone, with music from the 1950s, 60s and 70s, Motown, karaoke, discos and excellent, wholesome food too. Senior citizens appreciate a 2 course lunch on Thursdays for £3.95. *Opposite the recreation ground.*

The Unicorn (2)
Church Lane
Trumpington

☎ 01223 845102
Location:

Dating to 1845, this is one of Cambridge's oldest pubs and has excellent car parking facilities. Delightful fresh home cooked food, such as pizzas, oven roasted jacket potatoes, juicy steaks and spicy curries, available all day Friday-Sunday. Children love the ever popular bouncy castle. *Just outside Cambridge on the A10, a few miles from the M11.*

Waggon & Horses
High Street
Newmarket

☎ 01638 662479
Location:

The place to be seen in Newmarket! New landlord, Fran O'Brien has made dramatic changes here. He offers excellent food, such as roast of the day, home-made steak & Guinness pie and chicken Stroganoff, plus 6 well kept real ales. Sky tv is available too, so you can watch live football matches and racing events. *Near the monument in the High Street.*

Wash & Tope Hotel
10-12 Le Strange Terrace
Hunstanton

☎ 01485 532250
Location:

Now run by Paul and Louise, this traditional seaside hotel has 10 guest rooms from £35, some with great sea views and there's a family room too. Open all day, the new menu features homely food like lamb shank and fresh fish & chips plus a good Sunday roast. Lots to do with live music and a games room with Sky tv. *In the heart of Hunstanton, facing the sea.*

Weeping Willow
39 Bury Road
Barrow

☎ 01284 810492
Location: (EC P.181)

This grade II listed pub has 2 inglenook fireplaces and, of course, a willow tree in the garden! Now run by Sue and Sean who have brought a touch of Dublin to Suffolk! The French chef has created a delightful weekday a la carte menu plus a fantastic carvery served all day Saturday and Sunday. Kids bouncy castle. *Centrally located.*

The West End
43 Long Lane
Feltwell

☎ 01842 827711
Location:

A pleasant, country pub, owned by the Ewen family who provide good English pub food and Greene King real ales, as well as their own-label wine. A family atmosphere with a super carvery 5 times a week, complete with home-made Yorkshire puddings! Functions, outside bars and many special meal deals. *West side of the village.*

White Hart (1)
2 London Road
Swaffham

☎ 01760 723333
Location:

Under new management and recently refurbished, this lively venue is open all day and has plenty to offer. Discos on Thursdays and Fridays, live music on Saturdays as well as Sky tv, pool and a video jukebox. Relax in the garden in summer and enjoy tasty snacks like sandwiches, baguettes and basket meals. *By the Market Place.*

White Hart (2)
10 High Street
Tuddenham

☎ 01638 713061
Location:

An excellent range of food is served here, from Mexican chilli and giant filled Yorkshire puddings to a weekly special authentic Thai dish. You must try the amazing monthly Thai banquet too! Good entertainment as well, with live music, karaoke, theme nights and pub games include pool, darts, crib and dominoes. *On the High Street.*

White Hart Bar
& Restaurant
1 Balsham Road
Fulbourn
☎ 01223 880264
Location: (EC P.155)

A well established venue on the outskirts of the historic city of Cambridge. New tenants, Philip & Amanda Wharrier are making subtle improvements, whilst retaining the already successful formula. A wide choice of food, from snacks to a la carte and the ever popular carvery. 7 en suite rooms from just £45 B&B. *Close to the A11, on the edge of the village.*

White Horse (1)
118 High Street
Barton

☎ 01223 262327
Location: (EC P.164)

This delightful C18th, beamed pub has a roaring fire and boasts 2 en suite guest rooms. Fabulous, home-made food is served all day, from simple snacks to a full a la carte menu, and is available in both the bar and the non-smoking restaurant. Lovely garden for the summer and sited close to Cambridge and Wimpole Hall. *Opposite the garage.*

White Horse (2)
22 High Street
Milton

☎ 01223 860327
Location: (EC P.181)

This pretty C16th building has all the traditional English style you might expect but with a light and modern interior. The food is mainly British, with a children's menu too, and there are 4 good ales to sample. The large garden with a kids' play area is ideal for families. Thursday quiz and entertainment on Fridays. *In the centre of the village, 1/2 a mile from the A14.*

White Horse (3)
Longstanton Road
Oakington

☎ 01223 232417
Location: (EC P.166)

This Mexican themed pub has a heated patio and a beautifully manicured garden with a play area for the kids. New tenants, Karen & Tony have improved the Mexican menu by adding daily specials and now offer a fantastic Sunday roast, available from 12-6pm. Floodlit petanque, giant Connect 4 and darts. *In the centre of the village.*

White Horse (4)
Rede Road
Whepstead

☎ 01284 735542
Location: (EC P.156)

A delightful, traditional country pub located just a few miles from historic Bury St Edmunds. 3 well kept real ales and delicious, wholesome food from steak & kidney pudding and steaks to home-made curries. Dating from 1700s, with a real fire and a large garden, this is a lovely venue for the whole family. *5 miles south of Bury St Edmunds in the centre of the village.*

White Horse Inn
White Horse Street
Brandon

☎ 01842 815767
Location:

Now run by David and Jeni, who provide a friendly and homely atmosphere. Open all day, they have introduced a nice bar menu, such as scampi & chips and fresh Ploughman's salads, and serve 2 real ales. There's a large garden for the summer months, plenty of pub games and monthly entertainment. *1/2 a mile from the centre, set behind the main road.*

Area 4

Bedford, Sandy, Biggleswade, Newport Pagnell,
Bletchley, Milton Keynes, Woburn, Leighton Buzzard,
Dunstable, Luton, Hitchin, Stevenage, Baldock
and surrounding areas.

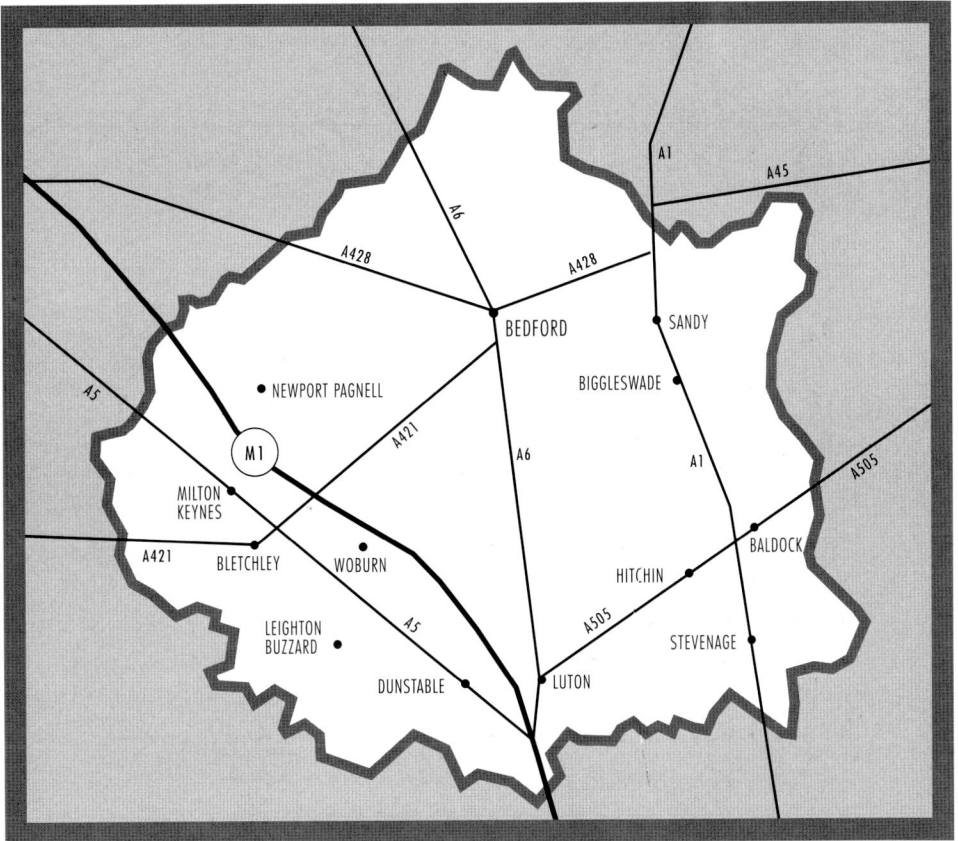

Establishment	Nearest Town	Page No.	Waterside Setting	All Day Opening	Pets Welcome	Takeaway	Real Ales	Rooms From £	No. Bedrooms	Baby Changing	Child Portions	Play Area	Garden	No. of Covers	Average Price	Vegetarian Food	Credit Cards	Functions	Live Music	Coaches Welcome	Air Conditioning	No Smoking	Disabled Access
Akash Tandoori	Bedford	74			•	•						•	•	40	8	•	•	•	•		•	•	•
Bedford Arms (1)	Dunstable	74			•	•	2					•	•	40	7	•	•	•	•	•			•
Bedford Arms (2)	Rushden	74			•	•	2					•	•	80	7.95	•	•	•				•	•
Bell Inn	Dunstable	74			•		4					•	•	50	7	•	•	•	•	•	•	•	•
The Bombay	Stevenage	74			•	•						•	•	76	5	•	•	•			•	•	•
The Bramingham	Luton	74			•		2				•	•	•	90	6	•	•	•	•	•		•	•
Bucks Head	Stevenage	75			•		2				•	•	•	60	9.50	•	•	•	•				•
The Castle	Bedford	75			•		4	25	4		•	•	•	60	5.50	•	•	•	•			•	•
The Chequers	Rushden	75			•		5					•	•	40	8.50	•	•	•	•	•		•	•
City Limits	Milton Keynes	75				•						•		250	9	•	•	•	•	•	•	•	•
The Cock Inn	St Neots	75			•		3			•	•	•	•	60	6.95	•	•	•	•	•			•
The Crown	Leighton Buzzard	75			•		2				•	•	•	40	10	•	•	•				•	•
Crown & Cushion	St Neots	76					4				•	•	•	40	5.95	•	•	•	•				•
Express Hol. Inn	Luton	76					1	55	75	•	•	•		60	8.50	•	•	•			•	•	•
Forester's Arms	Northampton	76					2	95	16			•		300	18	•	•	•	•		•	•	•
The Fox	Stevenage	76			•		3				•	•	•	25		•	•	•	•			•	•
Fox & Hounds	Stony Stratford	76					5				•	•	•	20	5	•	•	•	•				•
Gardners Arms	Biggleswade	76			•		1				•	•	•	40	5.50	•	•	•	•			•	•
Golden Lion	Biggleswade	77					1				•	•	•	30	4.50	•	•	•	•				•
Hermit of Redcoats	Stevenage	77			•		4				•	•	•	24	5	•	•	•	•			•	•
Horse & Groom	Bedford	77			•		3				•	•	•	70	7	•	•	•				•	•
Il Forno Italian R.	Baldock	77									•	•	•	75	7	•	•	•			•	•	•
Jainbi Seafood R.	Bedford	77				•					•		•	40	10	•	•	•			•	•	•
Jolly Coopers	Flitwick	77									•	•	•	64	9	•	•	•	•			•	•
Kingston Tavern	Milton Keynes	78		•	•	•	2				•		•	46	7.95	•	•	•	•			•	•
Lynmore	Ampthill	78			•						•			170	7	•	•	•			•	•	•
Mama Rosa's	Leighton Buzzard	78					3				•			80	10	•	•	•			•	•	•
	Leighton Buzzard	78									•			80	8	•	•	•				•	•

72

Name	Nearest Town	Page No.	Waterside Setting	All Day Opening	Pets Welcome	Takeaway	Real Ales	Rooms From £	No. Bedrooms	Baby Changing	Child Portions	Play Area	Garden	Average Price	No. of Covers	Vegetarian Food	Credit Cards	Functions	Live Music	Coaches Welcome	Air Conditioning	No Smoking	Disabled Access
McDonalds	Milton Keynes	78		•							•	•	•	3.60	50	•	•	•		•	•	•	•
Meah Tandoori R.	Luton	78			•									9	60	•	•	•		•	•		•
Mother Red Cap	Luton	79		•			3						•	3.50	35	•	•	•	•	•		•	•
Musgrave Arms	Hitchin	79				•	2			•	•	•	•	8	50	•	•	•					•
New French P'dge	Northampton	79							10		•			12	50	•	•	•				•	•
Park Hotel	Bedford	79		•			3		140		•			8.75	84	•	•	•		•		•	•
Pizza Express (1)	Milton Keynes	79		•						•	•			6.50	190	•	•					•	•
Pizza Express (2)	Hitchin	79		•						•	•			7	145	•	•					•	•
The Priory Roast	Dunstable	80					2						•	7	90	•	•	•		•		•	•
Quality Hotel	Milton Keynes	80		•			4	50	88		•			15	90	•	•	•	•	•	•	•	•
The Racehorse	Huntingdon	80		•		•	2	44	5		•	•	•	8	120	•	•	•		•			•
The Red Lion	Nebworth	80	•	•			3				•		•	4	60	•	•	•		•		•	•
The Rising Sun	Luton	80				•					•		•	5	40	•	•	•					•
The Royal George	Bedford	80		•		•	2				•			9	24	•	•	•		•			•
The Royal Oak (1)	Bedford	81	•			•	1				•		•	5	30	•	•						•
The Royal Oak (2)	Woburn	81		•			4				•		•	6.50	40	•	•	•				•	•
St Albans Hotel	St Albans	81		•				38	15		•			15	40	•	•	•		•		•	•
Studi L. C. & W.B.	Bedford	81												4	40	•	•	•					•
Super Cook C.R.	Sandy	81		•							•			6	45	•	•					•	•
Taste of India	Stevenage	81			•									8	36	•	•	•		•			•
Three Horseshoes	Bedford	82		•			2				•	•	•	6	38	•	•	•		•		•	•
The Wheatsheaf	Milton Keynes	82		•			2				•		•	8.50	18	•	•	•					•
The White Hart	Bletchley	82		•			2				•			5.99	75	•	•	•		•		•	•
White Horse	Woburn	82		•			1				•		•	5	36	•	•	•					•
Woodlands Manor	Bedford	82		•				59.50	33	•	•			20	50	•	•	•	•	•	•	•	•
Yorkshire Grey	Biggleswade	82		•			1			•	•	•	•	5.50	100	•	•	•		•			•

Akash Tandoori Restaurant
2-3 Springfield Centre
Kempston
☎ 01234 851133
Location:

This fresh, modern styled restaurant is adorned with abstract artwork and boasts its own car park. Enjoy delicious, authentic dishes like lamb Laziz and classic Indian food such as chicken Passanda. Disabled friendly, sample tasty food at home too by benefiting from the efficient takeaway and delivery service. *1 mile from the town centre.*

Bedford Arms (1)
High Street
Toddington

☎ 01525 873503
Location:

Set in nearly 2 acres of grounds, this country establishment has bags of old-fashioned charm enhanced by 2 open fires. Here, Amanda and Chris offer a choice of ales and large portions of good, traditional cooking like lamb shank and Cajun chicken. A relaxed environment where you can watch for the friendly ghost! *At the top of the High Street.*

Bedford Arms (2)
High Street
Souldrop

☎ 01234 781384
Location:

Simon & Becky boast a warm atmosphere at their friendly pub, complete with open fires. They offer a changing menu of home-made dishes, prepared from fresh, local produce, such as cod in beer batter, sausage & mash and steak & kidney pie. Family orientated, with a car park, pretty garden and a new play area. *In the middle of the village.*

Bell Inn
Dunstable Road
Studham
Nr Dunstable
☎ 01582 872460
Location:

This delightful, C16th pub is an ideal place in which to relax after a visit to Whipsnade Zoo. The spectacular views from the garden, complete with patio heaters, have to be seen to be believed, providing a wonderful backdrop for summer barbecues and beer festivals. Super food prepared by qualified chefs. *Off the A5 through Kensworth.*

The Bombay
77-79 High Street
Stevenage

☎ 01438 314699
Location: (EC P.189)

This is the oldest Indian restaurant in Stevenage, yet it has been refurbished in a modern and contemporary style with unique artwork adorning the walls. High quality, fresh Bangladeshi, Indian and Nepalese cuisine is served with a 5 course gourmet menu every Tuesday night for just £9.95. Ideal for functions. *In the middle of the High Street.*

The Bramingham
Quantock Rise
Bramingham Park
Luton
☎ 01582 616767
Location:

An extensive and delicious bar menu is served here with mouthwatering dishes like home-made chilli, fresh lasagne and juicy steaks. The atmosphere is friendly and lively with bands every month and regular summer barbecues. 2 well kept real ales, a large car park and the garden is secure for children to play in. *Beside Sainsburys.*

Directory

Bucks Head
Stevenage Road
Little Wymondley

☎ 01438 353320
Location: (EC P.196)

This 400 year old pub has lots of character with old beams and an inglenook fireplace. Families are warmly welcomed and children appreciate their own menu and the garden with climbing frame. Good food available lunchtime and evening and a superb Sunday carvery. Lovely outside decking area for the summer. *0.6 of a mile from junction 8 of the A1.*

The Castle
17 Newnham Street
Bedford

☎ 01234 353295
Location: (EC P.192)

A traditional town pub that also boasts a garden, complete with outdoor heaters. Nice food, with steak & kidney pie, lamb steaks and home-made lasagne and good English desserts like Spotted Dick. Themed food evenings, superb wines and great beer, with Adnams, Broadside, Eagle IPA and Bombadier. *Off the town centre, 2 minutes walk from the river.*

The Chequers
High Street
Yelden

☎ 01933 356383
Location: (EC P.190)

You'll find a comfortable, homely atmosphere here, with real fires and a lovely terraced garden. Sample freshly prepared salads, succulent steaks and tempting liver & bacon, as well as mouthwatering desserts like Tiramisu and poached fruits. Great beer too, with 5 real ales, 2 real ciders and a May beer festival. *In the middle of Yelden.*

City Limits
Xscape
602 Marlborough Gate
Central Milton Keynes
☎ 01908 295207
Location:

Enjoy 2 venues in 1 place! Old Orleans on the first floor boasts delightful food, such as Cajun chicken, Jambalaya and Alabama fudge cake, and fabulous balcony dining, whilst on the ground floor is The First Base Sports Bar with a lovely courtyard. Open all day, with live music on Thursdays and Sundays. *Central Milton Keynes.*

The Cock Inn
25 Church Street
Gamlingay

☎ 01767 650255
Location: (EC P.195)

New landlord, Jerry & Nicole Beasty class this as a 'proper pub', as it has been for over 400 years! 3 real ales and an interesting range of food, such as beer battered cod, succulent steaks and a delicious, home-made bread & butter pudding. A homely atmosphere with a lovely inglenook fireplace. *2 minutes walk from the church.*

The Crown
72 North Street
Leighton Buzzard

☎ 01525 217770
Location:

Now managed by Nathan Naidoo, this traditional town pub serves a superb range of dishes on the lunchtime bar and evening restaurant menus. There is also a choice of home-made daily specials, an excellent Sunday roast and a new and improved international wine list. Good food and very generous portions. *200 yards from the town centre.*

75

Crown & Cushion
West Street
Great Gransden

☎ 01767 677214
Location:

This traditional village pub dates to the C15th and has oak beams, log fires and a pretty garden. It's an ideal venue to sample wonderful, country cooking, such as home-made steak & ale pie and sticky toffee pudding. Excellent entertainment on 3 nights of the week, with jazz, rock bands, discos and karaoke. *The only pub in the village.*

Express by Holiday Inn
Luton Hemel M1 J9
Flamstead
☎ 01582 841332
Location:

With easy access to local towns, the location of this popular hotel makes it an ideal venue for business or pleasure. Great value, with a family room priced at just £55 at weekends, and the adjacent Harvester restaurant catering for everyone. Modern facilities and excellent service provide for all business needs. *Junction 9 M1.*

Falcon Hotel & Restaurant
Castle Ashby

☎ 01604 696200
Location:

This multi award winning hotel & restaurant is over 400 years old and has a delightful country garden where fresh vegetables and herbs are grown for the kitchen. Choose from simple snacks to seasonal a la carte dishes. Private functions and corporate events are efficiently catered for. 16 en suite rooms from £95. *In the centre of the hamlet. www.falconhotel-castleashby.com*

Forester's Arms
Wolverton Road
Stony Stratford

☎ 01908 567115
Location:

New landlady, Sonia has created a jovial atmosphere for both males and females to enjoy. Excellent theme events are held once a month from 70s nights to fancy dress parties! Live entertainment too, every Thursday and Sunday, and pool and darts. 2 real ales have been introduced and an improved wine list. *In the heart of town.*

The Fox
New Road
Woolmer Green

☎ 01438 813179
Location:

A friendly, village pub, dating back to the C17th, offering a super selection of food prepared by fully trained chefs. Choose from simple snacks at lunchtime through to delicious Coq au Vin and pork with redcurrant sauce in the evenings. Monthly live music, weekly quiz, pub games and a choice of 3 real ales. *By the village pond.*

Fox & Hounds
87 High Street
Stony Stratford

☎ 01908 563307
Location:

Newly refurbished, this grade II, C18th pub serves fabulous food and 5 well kept real ales. Freshly made dishes are prepared from local produce, such as tiger prawns, succulent steaks, juicy burgers and crispy salads. Lots of music too, with live bands Thursdays and Saturdays and a Monday jamming session. *In the centre of town.*

76

Gardners Arms
37 Potton Road
Biggleswade

☎ 01767 315126
Location:

Formerly old cottages, this friendly pub has real fires and a secure garden with play equipment to keep the children happy whilst you can have a relaxing drink! Tracey & Paul serve good, old-fashioned basket meals like juicy burgers, fresh fish & chips plus jacket potatoes, baguettes and a great Sunday roast. *1/2 a mile from the centre.*

Golden Lion
Church Street
Clifton

☎ 01462 812392
Location: (EC P.188)

Now run by Sheila & Kevin, who have created a welcoming atmosphere with children loving the secure garden and play area. They serve good pub food such as steaming jacket potatoes and juicy burgers as well as super daily specials and a fabulous Sunday roast. Regular quiz nights and monthly entertainment. *1/2 a mile north of Henlow, in the middle of the village.*

Hermit of Redcoats
Titmore Green
Nr Little Wymondley

☎ 01438 351444
Location: (EC P.193)

This wonderfully named hamlet is near junction 8 of the A1. The pub is named after a centuries old eccentric aristocrat and today is run by Pam and Tony. They serve traditional English and international dishes and 4 real ales plus fresh fish & chips on Tuesdays. Regular summer barbecues. CAMRA commended. *Just off the A1 at junction 8, 2 miles south of Letchworth.*

The Horse & Groom
15 High Street
Clapham
Bedford
☎ 01234 217502
Location: (EC P.191)

This family run, C17th pub was formerly a coaching inn and boasts log fires for winter and an award winning riverside garden for summer. Wonderful food, made from local produce, like home-made onion rings and pate, freshly battered fish & hand cut chips, daily specials and a terrific Sunday roast. Please book. *Just off the A6, 2 miles north of Bedford.*

Il Forno
Italian Ristorante
48 High Street
Baldock
☎ 01462 491110
Location: (EC P.192)

Owned by Antonio Ciaravella who serves a superb a la carte menu of wonderful Italian dishes plus an extensive fish section from king prawns, mussels and scallops to sea bass and Dover sole. Complemented by fine wines from different regions of Italy, and good service, you will be very happy with your visit. *On the High Street.*

Jainbi
Seafood Restaurant
123 Midland Road
Bedford
☎ 01234 269999
Location:

This delightful restaurant offers a unique taste of Tropical and international cuisine, specialising in seafood but also providing a good choice of meat and vegetarian options. You can watch exciting dishes like Chicken Yasa and Tilapia fish cooked in the open plan kitchen and you can bring your own wine! *On the edge of the town centre.*

Jolly Coopers
Wardhedges
Near Flitton

☎ 01525 860626
Location:

This old-fashioned, country pub has a delightful garden and a paddock for the children to explore whilst you have a relaxing drink! There's a bar menu with favourites like fresh cod & chips and steak & ale pie, and a dining room menu with succulent steaks and 5 speciality sausages - try the wild boar and apple! *A mile east of Flitton.*

Kingston Tavern
Brewster's
Winchester Circle
Kingston, M. Keynes
☎ 01908 584371
Location:

Under new management, and refurbished to give a modern and bright environment, this popular Brewster's now has an excellent atmosphere. Kids will have great fun in 'The Fun Factory' and they can also choose from their own menu. Open all day, this is an ideal venue for the whole family. *In the Kingston Retail Park.*

Lynmore
Sharpenoe Road
Sharpenhoe

☎ 01582 881233
Location:

This delightful free house boasts a 'gastro' menu with simple yet delicious snacks such as fresh mussels, an a la carte menu and a speciality board with outstanding creations prepared from fresh ingredients. Try poached sole stuffed with salmon mousse or succulent fillet steak marinated in red wine and juniper berries. *Centrally located.*

Mama Rosa's Italian
Ristorante & Pizzeria
3 North Street
Leighton Buzzard
☎ 01525 375149
Location: **(EC P.189)**

A great choice of venue for a family meal, dinner with friends or a romantic supper. The extensive Italian menu features fresh pasta dishes, sumptious pizzas, crispy salads and the wonderful Mama Rosa fillet steak, complemented by Italian beers and a good choice of wines. Delightful garden for the summer too. *In the centre.*

McDonalds Restaurant
The Westcroft Centre
Barnsdale Drive
Milton Keynes
☎ 01908 501471
Location:

This popular family restaurant boasts a patio for alfresco dining and a drive through if you're in a hurry. The extensive menu includes all the traditional favourites and a new range of healthy breakfasts and salads. Now open from 6.30am-11pm, you'll experience fast and efficient service and fresh, high quality food. *2 miles from Central Milton Keynes.*

Meah Tandoori
Restaurant
102 Park Street
Luton
☎ 01582 454504
Location:

A reputable restaurant serving a superb range of Indian and Bangladeshi cuisine. Owner, Mr Zeaur Rahman offers delicious business lunches, great value at just £5.50 for 3 courses, and an astonishing Gourmet Night on Tuesdays for £7.95. There's a function room available, a takeaway service and free delivery. *Close to the council car park.*

78

Mother Red Cap
80 Latimer Road
Luton

☎ 01582 730913
Location: (EC P.187)

A friendly, town pub with a country atmosphere! Now run by Mike & Janet who have introduced a nice selection of food like home-made Shepherd's pie and a fantastic Sunday roast served all day; great value at only £4. There's a new beer garden and lots going on with discos, karaoke, quiz nights, pool and Sky tv. *Opposite Matalan.*

Musgrave Arms
16 Apsley End Road
Shillington

☎ 01462 711286
Location: (EC P.186)

Claire & Andy Dodd have vastly improved the food at this traditional village pub, serving home cooked dishes like steaks, fresh fish, game pie and a mouthwatering bread & butter pudding. An excellent Sunday roast too, senior citizens lunch on Thursdays and 2 cask ales to try in front of the open fires. *6 miles northwest of Hitchin on the edge of the village.*

The New French Partridge Hotel
Newport Pagnell Road
Horton
☎ 01604 870333
Location:

Awarded with 2 AA rosettes, this unique, former coaching inn serves the highest standard of English and French cuisine. Enjoy a quiet drink and tasty tapas in the Cellar Bar, or opt for a light snack or amazing delights from the a la carte menu. With 10 guest rooms, this is a superb venue for weddings and parties. *In the centre of the village.*

Park Hotel
98 Kimbolton Road
Bedford

☎ 01234 409305
Location:

New managers, Sarah and Darron serve a fantastic menu of traditional dishes, with a contemporary twist, and specialise in game. Food is served all day and you can have anything from a simple snack to wild mallard! There are real fires for you to relax by, and you must try the acoustic nights on Wednesdays. *Opposite Bedford Park.*

Pizza Express (1)
396-398 Midsummer Boulevard
Central Milton Keynes
☎ 01908 231738
Location:

Established in 1965, this British company, originating in Soho, is an expert in the preparation of authentic Italian pizzas. The ingredients are specially imported from Italy so you are ensured fantastic tasting food to add to your complete dining experience. Nicely refurbished function room for up to 35 guests. *In the heart of the shopping centre.*

Pizza Express (2)
19 Market Place
Hitchin

☎ 01462 450596
Location:

Open every day from 11.30am, this popular Italian restaurant serves fantastic pizzas and pasta dishes, fresh salads and an array of tempting appetizers and sweets, like marinated olives and delicious Banoffee pie. Parties up to 40 are most welcome and you can book in advance. Excellent jazz nights on Tuesdays. *On the Market Place.*

The Priory Roast
High Street North
Dunstable

☎ 01582 661530
Location: (EC P.187)

Now run by Russell & Debbie who have vastly improved the menu and are now offering an extensive range of home-made food. Choose simple snacks like paninis and juicy burgers or indulge in succulent steaks and fresh pastas. Renowned for their carveries on Wednesdays & Thursdays. Please book. *In the High Street.*

The Quality Hotel
Monks Way
Two Mile Ash

☎ 01908 561666
Location:

Newly refurbished to offer 88 en suite guest rooms, including 12 with stunning views of Abbey Hill golf course, and 6 rooms for corporate use. Excellent leisure facilities and a seasonal menu, from simple snacks to delicious a la carte cuisine, make this a super venue for business functions or pure indulgence! *Just off the A5/A422 intersection.*

The Racehorse Country Inn & Restaurant
43 High Street
Catworth
☎ 01832 710123
Location:

A lovely, traditional inn, with an open fire, adorned with horse memorabilia. David & Julie serve an array of home baked food, such as chicken wrapped in bacon with a mushroom sauce, and a super Sunday roast. There are 5 luxury bedrooms, all en suite and exceptionally clean, one with a jacuzzi bath to relax in! *Centrally located.*

The Red Lion
26 London Road
Woolmer Green

☎ 01438 813236
Location:

This family run pub serves good, traditional English food with an excellent carvery on Wednesdays and Sundays. Great value too, with 2 people able to eat lunch for £5 from Monday to Saturday lunchtimes. Children love the play area and the superb beer garden is ideal for the summer. Booking is advisable. *In the centre of the village, which is on the B197.*

The Rising Sun
1 Front Street
Slip End

☎ 01582 721766
Location:

Now run by Carol Diprose, this grade II listed pub dates to 1790 and has been given many refreshing changes. She serves a new and improved bar menu, daily specials and a Sunday roast. 2 for 1 specials will soon be on offer and you can enjoy 3 fine ales. Excellent patio for summer and functions are welcomed. *Beside the crossroads.*

The Royal George
High Street
Stagsden

☎ 01234 822801
Location: (EC P.191)

A quaint village pub with lots of character that welcomes everybody, including children and dogs! Bob and Alain serve good country cooking, using seasonal produce, such as home made quiche, fresh asparagus and mixed grills. Enjoy well kept real ales, fine wines by glass or bottle and have a go at skittles! *In the High Street.*

The Royal Oak (1)
33 High Street
Roxton

☎ 01234 870361
Location:

This traditional, village pub, complete with beams and real fires, is now run by Jemma Playford. She serves a lovely, varied bar menu, with a wholesome selection of traditional bar snacks as well as a delicious Sunday roast. Families are welcome and children will appreciate the garden which has a fine play area. *Off the A421 in the village centre.*

The Royal Oak (2)
40 George Street
Woburn

☎ 01525 290610
Location: (EC P.190)

Under new ownership, this grade II listed, C15th thatched pub now offers a superb choice of home-made food. Choose from simple, yet finely prepared bar meals like rustic sandwiches and steaming Shepherd's pie, or opt for classical French food, with a delightful and exciting 4 course table d'hote menu for £25. *On the edge of town, close to the A5 and M1.*

St Albans Hotel
3 Manor Road
St Albans
☎ 01727 853613
Fax: 01727 759115
Location:

Now under the ownership of Sylvia Inns, this delightful and friendly hotel is only a short walk from the town centre. It boasts its own beauty spa, which is open 10am-8pm and there are 15 well appointed bedrooms, including some for the disabled, from £38 including continental breakfast. *Near the train station. stalbans@ntlworld.co.uk*

**Studi Lounge Café
& Wine Bar**
33 St Cuthbert's Street
Bedford
☎ 01234 346870
Location:

Probably Bedford's trendiest café and wine bar, serving a wide choice of food and a good range of drinks. Try wholesome breakfasts, fresh baguettes, paninis and tempting tapas. Relax and enjoy a coffee or a glass of wine whilst watching Sky tv or the weekend live entertainment. Outside decking area too. *Opposite The Merton Centre.*

**Super Cook
Chinese Restaurant**
39 Tempsford Road
Sandy
☎ 01767 680288
Location: (EC P.188)

Sited in a former public house, the building is over 400 years old yet the restaurant has been refurbished with a modern outlook and style. Offering a fresh, Oriental menu with delights like Chinese crispy lamb and Thai seafood, there's also a takeaway menu plus free delivery within 5 miles. Open 7 days from 5pm. *On the A1 north, a mile from the town centre.*

**The Taste of
India Restaurant**
48A High Street
Stevenage
☎ 01438 720333
Location:

Experience authentic Indian cuisine in a modern environment. Dine on a wide variety of dishes, from Indian fish and vegetarian options as well as the classic meat curries, plus there's a super offer of a starter, main course and side dish, all for just £7.95. Open every day with a takeaway and free delivery service. *In the centre of the old town.*

Three Horseshoes
42 Top End
Renhold
Nr Bedford
☎ 01234 870275
Location:

Now run by Paula and Mark Brown who have refurbished throughout as well as introducing a non-smoking bar area. They serve a good, traditional English menu of home-made fayre, including delicious pies and desserts. There's a choice of 2 real ales and the secure, large beer garden hosts barbecues in summer. *In the centre of the village.*

The Wheatsheaf
Mount Pleasant
Aspley Guise

☎ 01908 583338
Location: (EC P.194)

Now run by Susie Manning who is focusing on home-made food, with traditional dishes such as delicious liver & bacon casserole and steak & kidney pie. Open all day, the kids will love the play area in the garden, and there's also a field for caravanners and campers. 2 good real ales, table skittles, darts and dominoes. *2 miles from the M1, on the edge of the village.*

The White Hart
Hungry Horse
Whaddon Way
Bletchley
☎ 01908 372965
Location:

This family friendly pub serves the popular Hungry Horse menu with traditional favourites such as succulent steaks and fine burgers plus a range of fresh salads. Lots of entertainment with karaoke on Fridays and discos or live music every Saturday, as well as pool and darts. Large garden with play area. *Off A5, 1 1/2 miles from the town centre.*

White Horse Inn
Kimbolton Road
Keysoe

☎ 01234 376363
Location: (EC P.193)

A traditional village local, complete with beams and real fires. Run by the Cinnamond family who serve Eagle Bombadier and IPA bitter and a nice selection of English classics like bangers & mash and fresh pies, as well as a choice of 10 desserts. Good theme nights, with curry, pims and cheese & wine evenings. *On the B660, 10 miles north of Bedford.*

Woodlands Manor Hotel
Green Lane
Clapham

☎ 01234 363281
Location:

Set in over 4 acres of wooded gardens, this country house hotel has 33 en suite rooms from £59.50. Relax by the real fires and sample a range of quality wines and enjoy the fine food. With 2 AA rosettes in both 2004 & 2005, you'll be astounded by the quality and passion of the Mediterranean and English cuisine. *Set back off the High Street.*

Yorkshire Grey
Hungry Horse
London Road
Biggleswade
☎ 01767 313222
Location: (EC P.194)

A fun venue for the family and now run by Barry & Wendy Robinson. They serve Greene King ales and the extensive 'Hungry Horse' menu featuring juicy steaks, Cod Almighty, as well as delicious English desserts. Your children will love the 'Pony Club' menu and games. *Beside the Registry Office.*

Area 5

Peterborough, Skegness, Boston, Donnington,
Grantham, Spalding, Wisbech, Stamford, Oundle, Huntingdon
and surrounding areas.

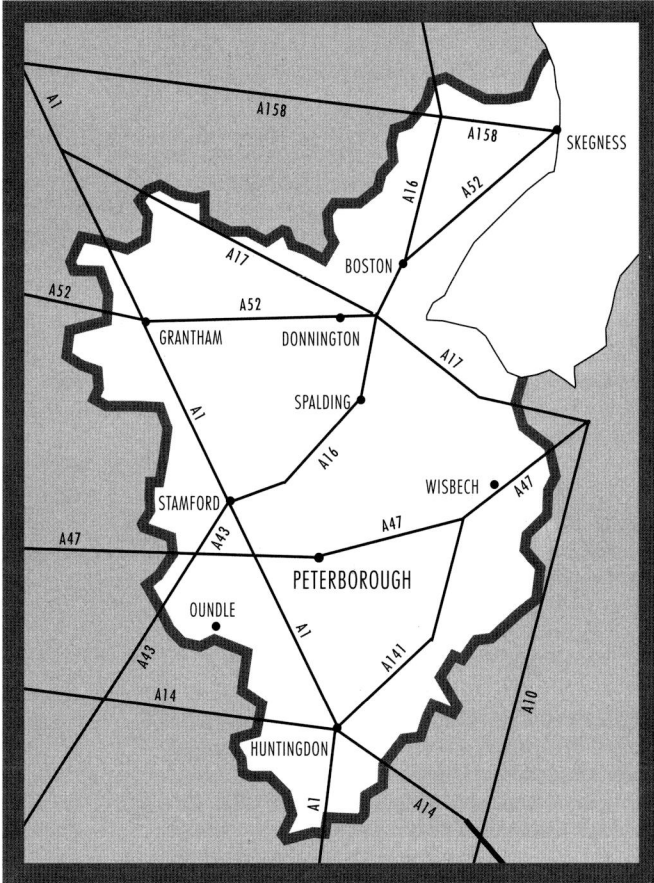

Establishment	Nearest Town	Page No.	Waterside Setting	All Day Opening	Pets Welcome	Takeaway	Real Ales	Rooms From £	No. Bedrooms	Baby Changing	Child Portions	Play Area	Garden	Average Price	No. of Covers	Vegetarian Food	Credit Cards	Functions	Live Music	Coaches Welcome	Air Conditioning	No Smoking	Disabled Access
Angel Inn	Oundle	87		●	●	●	3					●	●	5	35	●	●	●	●	●	●	●	●
Baskerville Hotel	Market Deeping	87		●	●		4	45	9				●	7	100	●	●	●	●	●		●	●
The Bell	Holbeach	87		●			1	25	6				●	1	12		●	●		●		●	●
Bell Inn	Spalding	87		●			3					●	●	7	30	●	●	●		●			●
B'field Wheatsheaf	Oundle	87		●				65	19			●	●	12	70	●	●	●	●			●	●
Berkley Arms	St Neots	87		●			2					●	●	5	50	●	●	●	●	●			●
Black Horse Inn	Bourne	88		●			3	45	6			●	●	9	80	●	●	●	●				●
Bluebell Inn	Peterborough	88		●	●		4					●	●	7.95	40	●	●	●					●
Blue Bell Inn	Peterborough	88		●	●		7					●	●	8	100	●	●	●					●
Bull Inn	Peterborough	88		●	●		3					●	●	6	60	●	●	●					●
Bulls Neck	Holbeach	88		●	●		2					●	●	8	60	●	●	●					●
China Palace R.	Bourne	88				●								8	50	●	●					●	●
Coopers	Peterborough	89		●			2					●	●	2.45	45	●	●	●	●				●
Cross Keys	Ramsey	89		●			3						●	8	50	●	●	●		●			●
Daniel Lambert	Stamford	89		●			5					●	●	6.50	60	●	●	●		●			●
Deep Pan Pizza Co	Skegness	89		●		●				●	●			6	120	●	●					●	●
The Dining Room	St Neots	89		●										6	30	●	●			●			●
The Falcon	St Neots	89		●			1			●	●			6	30	●	●						●
Finch Hatton Arms	Sleaford	90		●			3	44	8			●	●	6	55	●	●	●	●				●
Fox Inn	Yaxley	90		●			4					●		6.50	50	●	●	●		●			●
Garwick Café	Boston	90				●					●			4	50	●	●					●	●
George at Ramsey	Ramsey	90		●	●		1	45	11			●	●	9	70	●	●	●	●	●			●
Gordon Arms	Peterborough	90		●			2					●	●	7	18	●	●	●		●			●
Grand Hotel	Skegness	90	●	●				30	20					10	40	●	●	●	●	●		●	●
Gravity	Grantham	91		●								●		4	60	●	●	●	●				●
Greek Affair R.	Stamford	91		●	●	●								8	30	●	●	●		●			●
The Green Man	St Ives	91		●	●		3	25	5			●	●	6	42	●	●	●		●			●
Hero of Aliwal	Whittlesey	91	●	●	●	●	3					●	●	8	60	●	●	●		●		●	●

Speed Selector

	Nearest Town	Page No.	Waterside Setting	All Day Opening	Pets Welcome	Takeaway	Real Ales	Rooms From £	No. Bedrooms	Baby Changing	Child Portions	Play Area	Garden	Average Price	No. of Covers	Vegetarian Food	Credit Cards	Functions	Live Music	Coaches Welcome	Air Conditioning	No Smoking	Disabled Access
Hong Kong G.	Peterborough	91													40	•	•	•	•	•		•	
La Piazza	Skegness	91		•	•	•						•		•	68	•	•	•	•	•			•
Leeds Arms Hotel	St Neots	92		•	•			4		9		•	•	•	65	•	•	•		•			•
Lord John Russell	St Neots	92			•			4				•		•	35	•							•
Merrydale Hotel	Skegness	92				•		4	40	11		•		•	22	•	•		•				•
Mayfair Hotel	Skegness	92				•		4	20	8		•		•	20	•	•	•	•				•
Millstone Inn	Stamford	92				•		5	22		•	•		•	85	8.50	•	•	•	•			•
Nag's H. & Lesters	Bourne	92			•			2				•		•	106	4	•	•	•	•			•
Nags Head	Sleaford	93		•				2			•	•	•	•	32	4.90	•	•		•			•
The New Inn	Holbeach	93		•								•		•	32	6	•	•	•	•			•
New Kashmir Balti	March	93		•		•						•		•	80	4.50	•	•	•	•		•	•
Oriental Garden	March	93										•		•	90	8	•	•				•	•
Paper Mills	Stamford	93		•	•			2				•		•	50	12	•	•	•	•			•
Pig & Whistle	Swineshead	93		•				2				•		•	26	4	•	•	•	•			•
Plough Inn	Market Deeping	94						3				•		•	50	7.50	•	•	•	•			•
The Punchbowl	Stamford	94			•			3				•		•	30	5	•	•	•	•			•
Queen Inn	Spalding	94		•	•	•		3			•	•		•	32	7	•	•	•	•			•
Queens Head	Stamford	94						4				•		•	60	13	•	•	•	•			•
Red Lion Hotel	Skegness	94		•				2	22.50	6		•		•	50	6.50	•	•	•	•			•
Rico's Coffee Shop	Peterborough	95		•		•						•	•	•	75	5	•	•	•	•			•
Riverside Bar & R.	Kings Lynn	95		•	•	•			40	2		•		•	40	7	•	•	•	•			•
Rose & Crown (1)	Oundle	95		•			•	4				•		•	60	6	•	•	•	•			•
Rose & Crown (2)	Peterborough	95		•	•		•	4				•	•	•	50	10	•	•	•	•		•	•
Royal Mail Cart	Spalding	95						2				•		•	98	10	•	•	•	•			•
Royal Oak(1)	Bourne	95		•								•		•	20	5	•	•	•	•		•	•
Royal Oak (2)	St Neots	95		•	•			4				•	•	•	50	8	•	•	•			•	•
Saffron Indian R.	Holbeach	96			•		•								75	9	•	•	•	•		•	•
Seven Wives	St Ives	96		•		•		2				•	•	•	40	4.95	•	•	•	•		•	•

85

Name	Nearest Town	Page No.	Waterside Setting	All Day Opening	Pets Welcome	Takeaway	Real Ales	Rooms From £	No. Bedrooms	Baby Changing	Child Portions	Play Area	Garden	Average Price	No. of Covers	Vegetarian Food	Credit Cards	Functions	Live Music	Coaches Welcome	Air Conditioning	No Smoking	Disabled Access
Shanghai G'gdn (1)	Peterborough	96				•	•				•			40	7	•	•					•	•
Shanghai G'gdn (2)	Spalding	96			•											•	•					•	•
Singlecote Hotel	Skegness	96			•	•	•		10			•		26	5	•	•	•	•	•	•	•	•
Solstice Bar	Peterborough	96			•							•	•	150	4.50	•	•	•	•	•		•	•
South View Park H.	Skegness	97			•			2	19		•	•	•	62	10	•	•	•	•	•		•	•
Spinning Wheel	Market Deeping	97						4	22			•	•	60	9	•	•	•		•		•	•
Straw Bear	Whittlesey	97						2				•	•	48	5	•	•	•	•	•		•	•
Thatched Cottage	Boston	97			•	•		2			•	•	•	70	8	•	•	•				•	•
Toho Restaurant	Peterborough	97										•		300	22	•	•	•		•	•	•	•
Tollemache Arms	Melton Mowbray	97			•		•	3	4 30			•	•	50	10	•	•	•	•	•		•	•
The Towngate Inn	Market Deeping	98			•			4			•	•	•	42	11	•	•	•	•	•		•	•
Victoria Inn (1)	Huntingdon	98										•	•	30	8	•	•	•		•		•	•
Victoria Inn (2)	Skegness	98								•	•	•	•	100	7.65	•	•	•	•	•		•	•
Vine Hotel	Skegness	98			•		•		16		•	•	•	120	6	•	•	•	•	•		•	•
Wait for the W.	St Neots	98			•	•	•		20			•	•	60	5	•	•	•	•	•		•	•
White Horse Inn	Kimbolton	98			•	•	•					•	•	50	9	•	•	•	•	•		•	•
Windmill	Skegness	99									•	•	•	50	22	•	•	•				•	•
Windmill Tavern	Peterborough	99			•			9		•	•	•	•	100	8	•	•	•	•	•		•	•
Wishing Well Inn	Bourne	99			•		•	5	12		•	•	•	150	8	•	•	•				•	•
Ye Olde Bridge Inn	Peterborough	99			•		•	5	35			•	•	108	10	•	•	•		•		•	•
Yin Dee Thai R.	Peterboroug	99	•		•		•							45	8	•	•	•				•	•

86

Angel Inn
St Osyths Lane
Oundle

☎ 01832 273767
Location: (EC P.206)

A traditional pub, recently refurbished but still full of character with lovely low beams. The home cooked food is mainly English with a specials board that changes daily and Sunday lunch for just £4.25! For beer lovers there are 3 real ales including a regularly changing guest ale. Weekly quiz and fortnightly music. *Just off the Market Place, in the centre of Oundle.*

The Baskerville Hotel
99 Main Street
Baston

☎ 01778 560010
Location: (EC P.200)

A large, friendly hotel that provides first class food, drink and service. Choose simple snacks or delightful dishes from the a la carte menu, all home-made and freshly prepared, plus a carvery at weekends. Children are welcomed and enjoy the play area and there are 9 lovely, en suite guest rooms at competitive prices. *At the crossroads in the centre of the village.*

The Bell
21 High Street
Holbeach

☎ 01406 423223
Location:

Recently refurbished, this friendly local now has 6 bedrooms to let from just £25, which includes a full English breakfast. The new management open for coffee and snacks from 10am and offer negotiable prices on long term stays. Regular live music and karaoke every other week plus darts, dominoes and crib. *In the middle of the High Street.*

Bell Inn
High Street
Gosberton

☎ 01775 840186
Location:

A friendly, village inn that serves an excellent choice of real ales and a nice range of pub food. The Sunday lunch is great value at £5.95, or 2 courses for £7.95, and children are catered for too. Plenty to do with lots of pub games and there are live singers to entertain you once a month. Open all day Friday to Sunday. *In the centre of the village.*

The Benefield Wheatsheaf
Upper Main Street
Upper Benefield
☎ 01832 205400
Location:

A C17th coaching inn, set in a quiet location with panoramic views, tastefully refurbished to offer 19 contemporary, en suite rooms. A wonderful variety of English and Continental food, prepared from fresh produce and locally reared meat. Classed as a country hotel, this is an ideal venue for all types of function. *On the edge of the village.*

The Berkley Arms
1A Berkley Road
Eynesbury

☎ 01480 216262
Location:

A Victorian pub set in the heart of this lovely village, close to the camping site. Very family orientated, with a large and secure beer garden that incorporates a kids play area. Enjoy good, home cooked, seasonal food like summer salads and barbecues and winter stews and children have their own menu too. *In the centre, not far from the camping site.*

Directory

Black Horse Inn
Grimsthorpe
Bourne

☎ 01778 591247
Location: (EC P.199)

A perfect venue in which to base yourself to view all the local attractions (9 miles from Rutland Water, nestling under Grimsthorpe Castle). A lovely rustic building with 6 en suite rooms from just £45, 3 ever changing real ales and super food on the bar or full restaurant menus, utilising fine local produce. *7 miles from the A1, 4 miles west of Bourne.* www.blackhorseinn.co.uk

The Bluebell Inn
10 Woodgate
Helpston

☎ 01733 252394
Location: (EC P.207)

A lovely, traditional village pub with York stone flooring and real fires as well as a portrait of the poet John Clare and framed poems. Delicious food like Lincolnshire sausages and curries with a fantastic weekday lunchtime special of 2 courses for just £4.95. Families are welcome and kids even have their own room. *In the centre of the village.*

Blue Bell Inn
6 The Green
Werrington

☎ 01733 571264
Location:

New tenants, Mark & Iveta provide a friendly, yet professional service to everyone and pride themselves on offering fine dining at good prices. Sample fresh Billingsgate fish and a selection of traditional and international fayre and delicious mouthwatering desserts. 7 Elgood's real ales and monthly blues and jazz. *Just off the A15, in the village centre.*

Bull Inn
Thorney Road
Newborough

☎ 01733 810349
Location:

Refurbished throughout, this friendly pub is now run by Julie & Ray Ferris who have introduced a fantastic new menu. Choose from home-made soups, warming Cottage pie, succulent steaks and tempting desserts such as chocolate profiteroles and apple pie. Regular entertainment and a large beer garden for summer. *By the crossroads on the edge of the village.*

Bulls Neck
Penny Hill
Nr Holbeach

☎ 01406 422154
Location: (EC P.204)

Set in an idyllic hamlet, this traditional pub has been freshened up inside by new landlord Richard Harris. He serves delightful food, from tasty bar snacks to fantastic a la carte dishes such as Mediterranean lamb Wellington, and gorgeous desserts. The wine list has been extended and a winter guest ale has been introduced. *Signposted off the A17 at the Holbeach roundabout.*

China Palace Restaurant
11 South Street
Bourne

☎ 01778 423466
Location:

This new restaurant has a modern interior yet serves classic Oriental dishes of supreme quality. Enjoy traditional Chinese food, Chefs Specials and a fantastic Sunday lunchtime buffet where you can eat as much as you like. Good wine list, Oriental beers plus a takeaway menu so you can enjoy it all at home too! *In the centre at the crossroads.*

Directory

Coopers
32-33 Copeland
South Bretton
Peterborough
☎ 01733 263347
Location:

Now under the capable management of Gary Whitbread, this modern venue has a light and airy feel. You can buy a pint from just £1.85 and food is served all day with all dishes under £2.50. Don't miss the great curry night on Mondays and enjoy regular bands, karaoke and discos, plus Sky tv, jukebox, darts and pool. *A mile from the centre.*

Cross Keys
High Street
Upwood
Nr Ramsey
☎ 01487 813384
Location: (EC P.207)

A warm welcome and a relaxed, friendly atmosphere where the experienced chef caters for all tastes. The extensive menus are complemented by a choice of daily fish and meat specials which are freshly cooked to order using local produce. A large range of liquors and liqueurs plus a paddock play area for kids. *2 miles southwest of Ramsey, in the centre of the village.*

The Daniel Lambert
20 St. Leonards Street
Stamford

☎ 01780 755991
Location: (EC P.202)

Now run by Sarah and Hamish, who hold the 'Cask Marque' for their ales, which include 3 changing guest ales. Great food too, with light bites such as the Daniel Lambert burger and super dishes from the restaurant menu like braised lamb shank in a rosemary & honey sauce, as well as tasty seasonal specials. *Off the town centre to the east.*

Deep Pan Pizza Co
5 The Hildreds
High Street
Skegness
☎ 01754 764258
Location:

A completely non-smoking restaurant, with air-conditioning, that offers a fantastic Italian menu from fresh salads to a great range of pizzas and pasta dishes. The 'All You Can Eat Buffet' is good value at £5.99 for adults and £1.99 for kids and is available 7 days a week from 12-8pm. Takeaway service too. *In the town centre.*

The Dining Room
50-52 Market Square
St Neots

☎ 01480 215787
Location:

Open all day, the award winning chef produces a fantastic array of Modern British cuisine in a cheerful environment. Choose delights such as rack of lamb in a red wine sauce, goats cheese & leek tart and warm chocolate pudding. OAPs can dine for £6 and you can check out the menus at *www.the-dining-room.com. On the Market Square.*

The Falcon
9 New Street
St Neots

☎ 01480 371073
Location:

New landlady, Sian Doyle runs this traditional drinking pub in the centre of town. Smoking throughout, she provides a warm and friendly welcome and opens all day, every day. There's a good selection of drinks, including Greene King IPA, darts, a free jukebox and a fortnightly disco, plus a nice courtyard area. *Just off Market Street.*

89

Finch Hatton Arms
Main Street
Ewerby

☎ 01529 460363
Location:

The new owner of this delightful free house, Russell Lister, serves a super a la carte menu featuring home-made specials. Try freshly battered haddock, sweet & sour chicken and mouth watering Bakewell tart. The function room is ideal for parties and conferences up to 50 and there are 8 bedrooms from £44.
Centrally positioned.

Fox Inn
34 Manor Road
Folksworth

☎ 01733 240258
Location: (EC P.201)

This C17th free house and restaurant boasts a beamed interior and an inglenook fireplace. Now run by Graham Bond who has created delicious and interesting a la carte and bar menus. Choose from garlic prawns to a wonderful rack of lamb with mint jus. 4 well kept real ales, champagnes and over 80 wines to tempt you!
A mile west of the A1/A15 Yaxley exit.

Garwick Café
Boston Road
Heckington

☎ 01529 460504
Location:

New owners, John and Lynne Bowden serve a fantastic menu from classic breakfasts and light snacks, such as omelettes and jacket potatoes, to tasty curries and home-made steak pie dinners. Open from 7.30am, enjoy the clean and fresh atmosphere and look out for the new patio coming soon.
On the A17 between Sleaford and Boston.

**The George Hotel
at Ramsey**
65 High Street
Ramsey
☎ 01487 815264
Location:

Now run by Julie & Ian Cornthwaite who offer a fabulous variety of cuisine, from traditional bar snacks to super a la carte dishes such as mushroom ravioli and succulent lamb shank. Try the Oriental buffet on Thursdays and enjoy Sky tv and regular entertainment. 11 en suite bedrooms from £45 with breakfast.
In the heart of the town centre.

Gordon Arms
Oundle Road
Orton Longueville

☎ 01733 231374
Location: (EC P.199)

Completely refurbished, this pub is a lovely venue for relaxed dining. Choose from a vast range of dishes from open melt sandwiches to hand-made pies from Ireland, plus kids have their own menu too. Open all day, there's a good choice of wines and real ales and fantastic service to accompany your meal.
In the village centre.

Grand Hotel
14 North Parade
Skegness

☎ 01754 763804
Location:

Open all year round, this seafront hotel has 20 en suite guest rooms, including 8 with glorious sea views. Prices start from £30 including a full English or Continental breakfast, plus there are discounts for stays of 4 days or more. Enjoy a relaxing drink on the patio overlooking the sea or a delicious evening meal.
On the seafront, close to the town centre.

90

Gravity
8 Market Place
Grantham

☎ 01476 571660
Location:

Customers range from 18-80 years old who come to experience the fantastic DJs four nights a week, or simply to enjoy a pint which start from an incredible £1.30! Open all day and with a great atmosphere, there is a new and improved English bar menu plus blackboard specials and twice weekly drink promotions. *On the Market Place in the centre of town.*

Greek Affair Restaurant
9 St Mary's Street
Stamford

☎ 01780 757100
Location:

This new restaurant, run by Panos and Tracy, is adorned with fantastic Greek murals and has been refurbished with marble topped tables and metal chairs. Truly authentic Greek dishes are served, which can be complemented by Greek wines, beers or brandy. Come on Friday and watch the belly dancers! *Town centre.*

The Green Man
East Street
Colne
Nr St Ives
☎ 01487 840368
Location: (EC P.208)

Owners Phil and Teresa have made a host of improvements to this pleasant village local, including the addition of a lovely new restaurant. They serve good and varied home cooked food including a pleasing choice of daily specials, fine wines and real ales (which you can sample at 2 annual beer festivals). *5 miles northeast of St Ives, on the B1050.*

Hero of Aliwal
75 Church Street
Whittlesey

☎ 01733 203736
Location:

Situated next to a canal and close to fishing lakes, this is an ideal spot for walkers, boaters and fishermen. Now with new owners, there's a delicious range of old English food to try in the restaurant with non-smoking area, including a daily roast. Big car park and 5 well appointed, en suite rooms from £25. *400 yards from town centre.*

Hong Kong Garden
11B Market Street
Whittlesey

☎ 01733 205959
Location: (EC P.209)

Felix Chow and staff extend the warmest of welcomes at this centrally located restaurant. He has an extensive menu of 140 authentic Chinese dishes, with set menus from £12.50. A wide range of wines is available, including Great Wall wine! Open Wed-Sat noon - 1.30pm and Tues - Sun evenings. *In the centre of the village, close to the Market Place.*

La Piazza
Italian Restaurant
Vine Road
Chapel St Leonards
☎ 01754 871986
Location:

This new Italian restaurant, situated in this delightful seaside town, is expertly run by the Setaro family. Modernly styled, the walls are adorned with pictures of Italian cities. Choose from fresh pastas, a range of pizzas and classic meat dishes, complemented by famous Italian wines and bottled beers. *Beside the shopping area in the town centre.*

Leeds Arms Hotel
The Green
Eltisley

☎ 01480 880283
Location: *(EC P.202)*

This traditional, village inn, now run by Keith & Pat Moodey, boasts 9 pleasant guest rooms from just £40, including a super breakfast. Try delicious fresh food, such as sautéed king prawns, mushroom Stroganoff and poached smoked haddock in creamy caviar sauce. 4 real ales and a secure garden, ideal for families. *On the edge of the village, just off A428.*

Lord John Russell
Russell Street
St Neots

☎ 01480 390669
Location: *(EC P.197)*

This is like a village pub but set in the heart of town! The open fire adds to the cosy atmosphere and children are now allowed until 6.30pm. There's a good range of wholesome food from English breakfasts, which start at 9am, to homely casseroles and weekly specials. Try your hand at pool, darts or petanque. *Just off the town centre.*

Merrydale Hotel
13 Glentworth Crescent
Skegness

☎ 01754 766485
Location: *(EC P.200)*

Owners, Bob and Christine Charman have created a home from home atmosphere at this lovely hotel with 11 bedrooms. Prices start from £20 pp and include a fantastic full English breakfast. There's a licensed bar plus a relaxing lounge with satellite tv and daily newspapers. Rolls Royce hire available. *A short walk from the seafront.*

Mayfair Hotel
10 Saxby Avenue
Skegness

☎ 01754 764687
Location:

This clean and homely hotel has 8 lovely, en suite guest rooms, including 3 with excellent facilities for the disabled. Prices start from just £22 bed & breakfast plus there's the option of a 3 course evening meal for an amazing £8. Families are welcome, with super discounted rates for children and under 2s are free. *A 2 minute walk from the seafront and 5 minutes from town.*

Millstone Inn
Millstone Lane
Barnack

☎ 01780 740296
Location:

Not far from Burleigh House, this lovely pub dates to 1672 and boasts a wonderful bar menu of restaurant quality. Fresh fish day is on Thursdays, curry night on Fridays and with over 35 main dishes to choose from, you'll be spoilt for choice! 4 real ales, CAMRA recognised and a self contained function suite. *Just off the A1, south of Stamford, in the village centre.*

Nag's Head Free House
& Lesters Night Club
2 Abbey Road
Bourne
☎ 01778 393644
Location: *(EC P.209)*

A bright and modern free house where owner Andrew Binder has made many improvements. There is a choice of 5 real ales and a fine selection of home-made food, with daily specials and steak nights on Wednesday and Thursday. Wine and dine in style, then pop up to Lesters and dance the night away. *On the corner of the crossroads, in the centre of town.*

92

Nags Head
2 Grove Street
Great Hale
Nr Sleaford
☎ 01529 460437
Location:

This C18th pub has recently been refurbished and is now run by Gary & Tracy. They serve a good variety of home cooked meals, the highlight being fresh fish & chips on Fridays. Now open all day, they also arrange a variety of live music on Saturdays and a quiz on Fridays. Outside catering and bars available. *In the village centre.*

The New Inn
Holbeach St Marks

☎ 01406 701231
Location:

A delightful village pub, with real fires, that dates to 1850. Good pub food is served with delights such as succulent steaks, home-made curry and lasagne and chuffing hot chilli plus 2 well kept real ales. Lots going on, with pool matches, darts, dominoes and crib, as well as live music and regular karaoke and discos. *On the edge of the village.*

The New Kashmir
Balti House
Elwyn Road
March
☎ 01354 660449/650974
Location:

Probably the best Indian restaurant in March! Specialising in authentic Balti dishes, fresh ingredients are cooked in a wok for optimum healthiness and you must try the massive naan breads for 4 people. Enjoy a 3 course meal on Sundays for just £6.50 and take advantage of the free delivery service within 3 miles. *200 yards off the town centre.*

Oriental Garden
6 March Road
Guyhirn

☎ 01945 450570
Location:

A fine, air conditioned venue that serves classic Oriental cuisine from Peking, Canton and Malaysia. Try the spare ribs, crispy beef, Malaysian curries and of course the duck! The wine list is truly international and you can also sample Chinese beers. Open every day, there is an excellent buffet on Sunday noon-9pm. *Just outside the village on the A141.*

Paper Mills Inn
London Road
Wansford

☎ 01780 782328
Location: (EC P.210)

This C18th, air conditioned free house is now run by Peter and Virginia Robinson who guarantee the superb quality of both food and service. They serve food at lunch and in the evening, from a la carte and bar menus. The venison pie is a regular favourite and the Streaky Steak and Chicken Romantica are marvellous too. *Off the A1 northbound , between Peterborough and Stamford.*

Pig & Whistle
Market Place
Swineshead

☎ 01205 820295
Location:

Under new and enthusiastic management and, unsurprisingly, there's a collection of ceramic pigs on display! Excellent food, from light snacks to battered cod & chips and ice-cream sundaes. There's a nice patio for the summer, children are welcomed and you can enjoy pool, darts, jenga and a regular quiz night. *On the Market Place.*

Plough Inn
Main Road
Deeping St Nicholas

☎ 01775 630260
Location: **(EC P.204)**

Situated in one of the longest villages in England, this grade II listed pub has been nicely refurbished by the new proprietor. Great food too with a delicious Sunday roast, summer barbecues and weekly fish & chips and steak nights. The wine list has been improved and there are 2 well kept real ales including a guest. *On the A16, in the centre of the village.*

The Punchbowl
21 Scotgate
Stamford

☎ 01780 752834
Location:

New manager, Danielle Preston has created a warm atmosphere at this community pub that dates back to 1836, complete with natural stonework and a beautiful interior. She has introduced popular entertainment, with theme nights and live music twice a week. Nice food served Tuesday-Saturday lunchtimes. *Opposite The Bombay Cottage.*

Queen Inn
49 Station Street
Donington

☎ 01775 820281
Location:

Newly refurbished, this friendly pub is adorned with pictures of football stadiums. Fresh bar snacks are served all day and there's a delightful evening a la carte menu too. Try delights such as leek & mushroom Stroganoff and delicious fruit crumbles plus a great steak night on Wednesdays and a superb roast on Sundays. *In the heart of the village.*

Queens Head
Main Street
Bulwick

☎ 01780 450272
Location: **(EC P.203)**

This wonderful, C17th free house has just received a CAMRA gold award and will be entered for pub of the year in the Peterborough area. New owners, Geoff & Angela serve Shepherd Neame Spitfire and 3 guest ales. Good Modern British cuisine, a super roast lunch on Sundays and a fine selection of wines. *Opposite the church.*

Red Lion Hotel
33 High Street
Wainfleet

☎ 01754 880301
Location: **(EC P.210)**

Glenn and Maxine Alcock run this traditional pub, boasting 6 bedrooms from only £22.50 pp including a hearty breakfast. They serve a variety of British food, from creamy omelettes to juicy steaks and mouthwatering desserts, and there's a fantastic patio with parasols and tables for the summer months. *In the centre of Wainfleet.*

Rico's Coffee Shop
6A Rivergate Arcade
Viersen Platz
Peterborough
☎ 01733 891791
Location:

Open every day, this homely coffee shop, with local artwork for sale, has a delicious yet healthy menu, with everything freshly made to order. Choose from home-made soups, seasonal salads, filled jacket potatoes, chunky sandwiches and fresh ciabattas, to name a few of the delights. 7 flavours of tempting ice-cream too! *Close to Asda.*

94

The Riverside Bar & Restaurant
16 Bridge Road
Sutton Bridge
☎ 01406 351402
Location: (EC P.205)

A lovely location, sited next to the swing bridge, this super bar and restaurant is under new proprietorship. The new menus feature delicious bar snacks, great restaurant dishes plus daily specials and an excellent Sunday roast. Live entertainment at weekends and 2 B&B chalets, great value from just £39.95. *Beside the bridge.*

Rose & Crown (1)
Market Place
Oundle

☎ 01832 273284
Location:

A lovely pub that has a delightfully pretty garden for the summer months. There's a choice of 4 well kept real ales and super a la carte cuisine prepared from fresh, local produce. A good variety of entertainment too, with a disco every Friday and either karaoke or live music on Saturdays. Functions welcomed. *On the Market Place.*

Rose & Crown (2)
2 Wisbech Road
Thorney
Peterborough
☎ 01733 270546
Location: (EC P.211)

A large Victorian pub in 3 acres of grounds, including a garden and kids' play area. The 100 item menu is prepared to order by 3 highly skilled chefs and served in the public and lounge bars as well as the restaurant. All in all, this is a first class country pub. Excellent outside catering available. *On the crossroads, next to the traffic lights.*

Royal Mail Cart
1 01 Pinchbeck Road
Spalding

☎ 01775 722931
Location:

A large pub, now run by Karen Woodstock, that has a lovely beer garden and a bowling green. Enjoy delicious food, served in the modern, conservatory style restaurant, prepared by 2 super a la carte chefs. Don't miss the excellent fish and steak night on Fridays, followed by either live music, magicians or comedians! *On the edge of town, 5 minutes from the centre.*

Royal Oak (1)
74 North Street
Bourne

☎ 01778 422718
Location:

Formerly a cobblers, this traditional pub has a friendly atmosphere and is now run by Mark and Anne Cunnington. Open all day, there's a nice range of food from chip butties to wholesome bar snacks & Sunday lunch. The garden is delightful, kids are welcome plus there's pool, darts and dominoes. *On the north side of the crossroads.*

Royal Oak (2)
High Street
Hail Weston

☎ 01480 472527
Location:

Set in 3 acres of delightful gardens, this family friendly pub serves outstanding food from fresh seafood to mouthwatering calves liver and children appreciate their own menu too. There's a great choice of real ales and a new and extensive wine list from around the world. Regular theme nights and summer barbecues. *On the High Street.*

Saffron
Indian Restaurant
7 Fleet Street
Holbeach
☎ 01406 420044
Location:

This wonderful, Indian restaurant, adorned with modern art, has a fantastic menu of both classic and unique dishes, created by an award winning chef. Eat as much as you like for £7.95 at the Sunday buffet, available from 12-5.30pm. Open every day, with a good wine list, Indian beers and a popular takeaway menu too. *On the edge of town.*

Seven Wives
Ramsey Road
St Ives

☎ 01480 462180
Location:

Now run by Mick and Mandy who have created a friendly atmosphere for the whole family. Children have their own menu as well as having a play area in the garden which is also host to summer barbecues. Great bar food, from tasty snacks to juicy steaks, and you can have a private party for up to 70 people. *1/2 a mile from the main shopping centre.*

Shanghai Garden (1)
579-581 Lincoln Road
The Triangle, New England
Peterborough
☎ 01733 552211
Location: (EC P.212)

Indulge yourself with classic Oriental cooking of the highest quality, with lots of choice with fish being the house speciality. An a la carte men is served Friday to Wednesday evenings and on Thursday evening there's a lavish buffet. Set lunches served every day and there's a takeaway and outside catering service. *In the New England suburb.*

Shanghai Garden (2)
Unit 1
White Hart Market Place
Spalding
☎ 01775 719012
Location: (EC P.212)

Housed in a grade II listed building which is over 300 years old, this delightful restaurant serves exclusive, quality, Oriental cuisine. You must try the fabulous buffets for just £3.99 day and £7.99 in the evenings, as well as the classic restaurant menu. There's a takeaway service available and free delivery too. *In the town centre.*

Singlecote Hotel
34 Drummond Road
Skegness

☎ 01754 764698
Location: (EC P.211)

Just a stroll from the sea, you'll find this 10 roomed, family run, residential hotel. Owned by Ian and Valerie Nicholls, who boast 9 en suite rooms, with rates from just £19 per person, with breakfast. There is an optional evening meal for just £5 and other facilities include a licensed bar and secure parking. *Close to the seafront and the town centre, on the north side.*

Solstice Bar
Northminster Road
Peterborough

☎ 01733 560231
Location:

A popular venue for watching sports events with an 11 feet wide screen satellite tv so it as if you're at the match itself! The new menu features light lunchtime snacks and wholesome dishes in the evening plus an excellent Sunday carvery. Good entertainment from Thursday to Sunday with great live music. *On the edge of town, close to the Queensgate shopping centre.*

South View Park Hotel
Burgh Road
Skegness

☎ 01754 896060
Location:

This modern hotel offers superior accommodation at great value for money. Enjoy a changing menu of high quality a la carte dishes in a spacious and light restaurant, excellent leisure facilities and superb guest bedrooms. Civil wedding ceremonies and business conferences and functions are most welcome.
On the A15 south bound.

Spinning Wheel
Church Street
Baston

☎ 01778 560395
Location: (EC P.198)

Now run by Richard & Caroline who have a fantastic menu that utilises fresh, local produce to create high quality food. Try outstanding casseroles and delicious curries and a great 2 course Sunday lunch for £9.50. Refurbished throughout, there's a lovely atmosphere in which to relax and sample one of the 4 real ales.
Just off the A15, in the centre of the village.

Straw Bear
103 Drybread Road
Whittlesey

☎ 01733 203105
Location:

Now run by Vincent & Joanne, who provide a homely and family friendly atmosphere and they'll soon be offering a range of traditional English food. Open all day, there are 2 well kept real ales to sample, a super beer garden plus 2 pool tables, darts, a quiz night and Sky tv with the Premiership Plus package.
On the edge of the north side of town.

Thatched Cottage
Pools Lane
Sutterton

☎ 01205 460870
Location: (EC P.197)

The new, yet experienced owners have made some excellent changes to this idyllic, village free house. Choose from a range of menus, featuring English food with an intercontinental blend and benefit from high quality produce and efficient table service. Lovely garden, with a large rockery, ideal for summer time.
Opposite the green.

Toho Restaurant
New Road
Northminster
Peterborough
☎ 01733 314949
Location:

One of the largest Oriental restaurants in Europe, this unique venue serves a fine menu of traditional Chinese and Cantonese dishes. Relax in the spacious bar and enjoy the informal Bar Platter, fine wines or one of 72 cocktails! The first floor boasts a business and function suite and outside terrace.
Near to the Queensgate Shopping Centre.

Tollemache Arms
48 Main Street
Buckminster

☎ 01476 860007
Location:

A former Victorian coaching inn that has been refurbished to a high standard and welcomes families, pets and even horses! Excellent real ales, a super wine list and fabulous Modern British food with fresh fish and game very much in evidence. There are also 5 comfortable, en suite rooms, with a 4 diamond AA rating.
3 miles west of the A1.

The Towngate Inn
3 Towngate East
Market Deeping

☎ 01778 348000
Location:

With a large car park and a lovely function room, this is an ideal venue for all types of occasion from birthday parties to wedding receptions. Delicious food from light snacks to a full a la carte menu featuring fresh fish and tender steaks, plus a carvery on Sundays. 4 well kept real ales to sample including a guest ale.
Just off the roundabout at the A15/A16 split.

Victoria Inn (1)
52 Ouse Walk
Huntingdon

☎ 01480 453899
Location: (EC P.208)

One of 3 pubs under the umbrella of Phil & Teresa Beer. A short walk from the river and newly refurbished, giving the pub a clean and fresh look and a wonderful non-smoking restaurant. Traditional English food is served, with home cooking to the fore, and succulent steaks highlighted as a popular dish.
Close to the river.

Victoria Inn (2)
Wainfleet Road
Skegness

☎ 01754 767333
Location:

Under new management, this family orientated pub serves a good range of traditional meals such as mixed grills, succulent steaks and succulent, fresh pies. There are excellent promotions too, like 2 steaks for £10 and kids eat free, and plenty of fun with karaoke, discos, live music, comedians and pool knockout.
2 minutes from Morrisons supermarket.

Vine Hotel
South Road
Chapel St Leonards

☎ 01754 872228
Location: (EC P.213)

A traditional free house with excellent disabled facilities, owned by Shirley and Alan Creed. Superb food, with game and fresh fish much in evidence. The monthly food events include costume parties and the large function room is just perfect for all parties. Lots of live music and 16 bedrooms from £20 per person.
Close to the beach, on the south side.

Wait for the Waggon
13 Great North Road
Wyboston

☎ 01480 212443
Location: (EC P.206)

A friendly pub, with good car parking and within easy access of the A1. Lovely food is served, such as home-made curries, pies and freshly baked pizzas, plus lots of delicious desserts like jam roly poly and steaming apple pie. Childrens portions available and kids love the outside play area and the secure garden.
On the A1, on the edge of the village.

White Horse Inn & Wriggly Dragon II Rest.
2 Stow Road
New Town, Kimbolton
☎01480 860304
Location: (EC P.198)

The best of both worlds all rolled in to one - a wonderful English pub and an outstanding Chinese restaurant. Choose classic English bar snacks or authentic Chinese dishes with specialities like deep fried stuffed mushrooms and Oriental meat dumplings. Takeaway service too and free delivery available within 3 miles.
A mile from the town centre in the New Town.

Windmill
46 High Street
Burgh Le Marsh

☎ 01754 810281
Location: *(EC P.213)*

New owner, George Armstrong has completely refurbished this wonderful restaurant where you can enjoy a fabulous 3 course meal for £22. Indulge in delights such as crispy roast duck with a black cherry sauce followed by whiskey marmalade ice-cream. Open Tuesday-Saturday evenings and Sunday lunchtimes. *In the centre of the village on the A158.*

Windmill Tavern
29 Cherry Orton Road
Peterborough

☎ 01733 231554
Location: *(EC P.205)*

What a place! Robert & Chris Meek have gained a 'Cask Marque' for the quality of their real ales and have up to 9 per week. Stunning fresh food too, served in their homely restaurant, such as a tortilla basket filled with Cajun chicken & Caesar salad. Quiz on Thursday, Sunday carvery and Premiership Plus available. *Just off the A605, 2 miles from the centre.*

Wishing Well Inn
Main Street
Dyke
Nr Bourne
☎ 01778 422970
Location:

This charming, centuries old country inn, has an abundance of character and is set in a beautiful location. Renowned as one of Lincolnshire's finest inns, a visit here is a must. Family friendly, there is a superb choice of 5 real ales plus traditional food of the highest quality. 12 lovely, well equipped letting rooms. *Just off the A15, north of Bourne.*

Ye Olde Bridge Inn
The Common
Crowland

☎ 01733 210567
Location: *(EC P.203)*

This traditional free house is now owned by Hilary & Dennis Wilson who serve a delicious, changing menu of home-made food including a choice of 6 fresh fish dishes and a super Sunday roast. A few yards from the river, the pub has been tastefully refurbished. The pretty, new beer garden is enclosed for children. *Close to the river and 1/2 a mile from the centre of Crowland.*

Yin Dee
Thai Restaurant
31 Lincoln Road
Peterborough
☎ 01733 344223
Location:

Amazing Thai food is served here. Fresh ingredients are used and the dishes are traditionally prepared on the premises. Try classic red and green Thai curries, steamed sea bass in lemon sauce and the restaurant is famous for its authentic Tom Yum soup. Party bookings can be arranged plus a takeaway service as well. *Behind Westgate Car Park.*

Area 6

Lincoln, Barton-upon-Humber, Scunthorpe,
Grimsby, Caistor, Gainsborough, Retford,
Market Rasen, Louth, Mablethorpe
and surrounding areas.

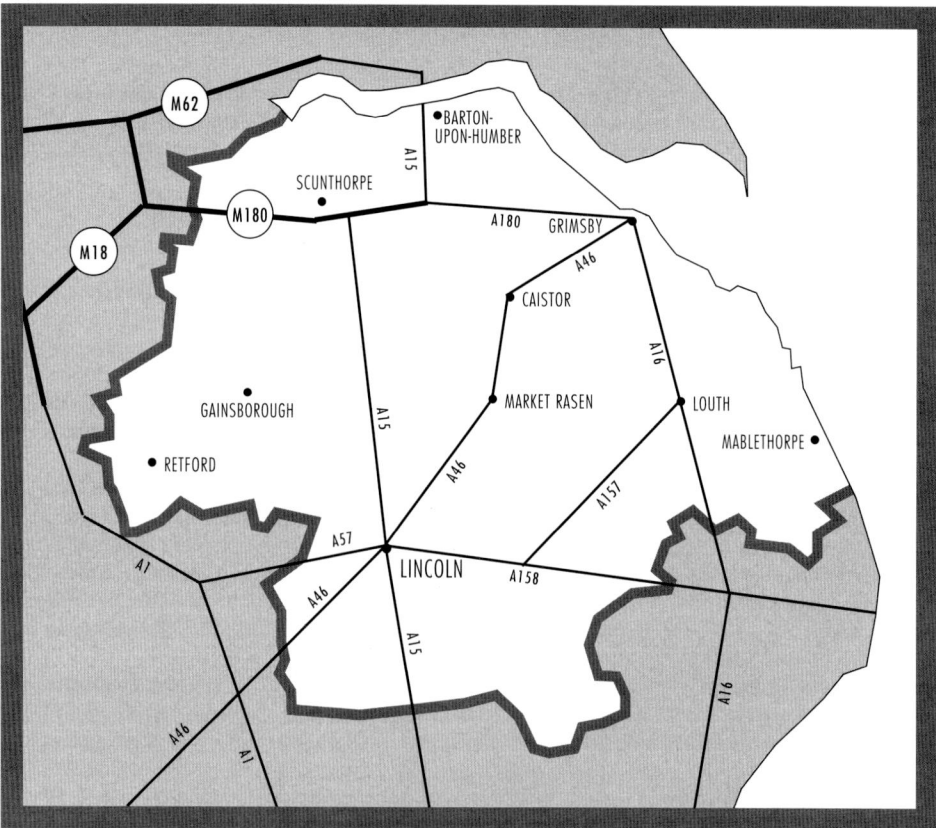

Establishment	Nearest Town	Page No.	Waterside Setting	All Day Opening	Pets Welcome	Takeaway	Real Ales	Rooms From £	No. Bedrooms	Baby Changing	Child Portions	Play Area	Garden	Average Price	No. of Covers	Vegetarian Food	Credit Cards	Functions	Live Music	Coaches Welcome	Air Conditioning	No Smoking	Disabled Access
Antimino's R.	Scunthorpe	104			•						•		•	11	50	•	•	•	•		•	•	•
Ashby Star Inn	Scunthorpe	104		•	•						•			3.25	45	•	•	•	•	•	•	•	•
The Attic Bar	Lincoln	104		•										6	60		•	•	•			•	•
Balti House R.	Cleethorpes	104			•	•							•	3.95	40	•	•	•					•
The Beach Bar	Mablethorpe	104	•		•	•					•			3	80					•			•
Black Horse (1)	Lincoln	104					5						•	7	40	•	•						•
Black Horse (2)	Alford	105					1																
Black Horse Cham.	Lincoln	105			•		2					•		14	40	•	•	•	•	•		•	•
The Black Horse I.	Louth	105					4						•	6	25	•	•		•				•
The Carnival Inn	Barton upon Humber	105		•																			•
Castle Hotel	Lincoln	105		•	•		1	19	67		•		•	9	40	•	•	•	•	•		•	•
City Vaults	Lincoln	105		•			2						•	5	60			•	•	•			•
Cromwells R.	Woodhall Spa	106			•								•	10	40	•	•				•		•
Cross Keys Inn	Louth	106		•	•		3				•		•	6.50	56	•	•	•		•			•
Don Giovanni R	Lincoln	106		•									•	10	120	•	•	•	•				•
Durham Ox	Horncastle	106			•		2							6.95	50	•	•						
Dynasty Chinese R.	Scunthorpe	106				•						•		6.50	60	•	•						•
Ebrington Arms	Horncastle	106		•			5						•	7.95	60	•	•		•				•
Epernay R.	Lincoln	107												17	60	•	•						•
The Fairways GC.	Woodhall Spa	107	•	•	•		3	20	75		•		•	7	50	•	•	•		•		•	•
Fleece Inn	Grimsby	107		•	•		3	3	22				•	7.50	60	•	•	•	•				•
Food For Thought	Lincoln	107			•									2.95	30	•	•					•	•
George & Dragon	Spilsby	107		•	•		3					•	•	5.95	66	•	•	•		•			•
The Glass House	Lincoln	107		•										6	140	•	•				•		•
The Haywain	Alford	108		•			2	19	32.50					7	50	•	•		•				•
The Homestead	Lincoln	108		•				190					•	7		•	•						•
Hope & Anchor	Barton upon Humber	108		•	•		3			•		•	•	8	100	•	•	•	•	•		•	•
The Juice Bar Cafe	Lincoln	108		•		•								3.50	34								•

101

Establishment	Nearest Town	Page No.	Waterside Setting	All Day Opening	Pets Welcome	Takeaway	Real Ales	Rooms From £	No. Bedrooms	Baby Changing	Child Portions	Play Area	Garden	Average Price	No. of Covers	Vegetarian Food	Credit Cards	Functions	Live Music	Coaches Welcome	Air Conditioning	No Smoking	Disabled Access
Kind Bar & R.	Lincoln	108		•							•	•	•	5.50	35	•	•	•	•	•		•	•
Kings Arms	Retford	108		•			2	42	11				•	10.50	45	•	•	•	•	•		•	•
Landings Hotel	Grimsby	109		•	•						•		•	10	200	•	•	•	•	•		•	•
The Lifeboat Bar	Cleethorpes	109		•		•					•		•	6	50	•	•	•	•	•		•	•
The Lynton	Cleethorpes	109		•	•	•	1				•		•	4.45	90	•	•	•	•	•		•	•
Mariners Rest	Grimsby	109		•	•	•	2				•		•	4	50	•	•	•	•	•		•	•
The Market Hotel	Retford	109		•	•	•	8			•	•		•	8	100	•	•	•	•	•		•	•
Masons Arms	Retford	109		•							•		•	5	50	•	•	•	•	•		•	•
Masons Arms H.	Louth	110		•			6	30	10		•		•	6	60	•	•	•	•	•		•	•
The Mayflower	Immingham	110		•			1				•		•	4.50	40	•	•	•	•	•		•	•
Mermaid Inn	Mablethorpe	110		•	•	•	2				•		•	5	80	•	•	•	•	•		•	•
Mill House Elms H.	Retford	110		•		•	2	50	19		•		•	8	60	•	•	•	•	•		•	•
My Father's M.	Louth	110		•			2				•		•	5	100	•	•	•	•	•		•	•
The Nags Head	Barton upon Humber	110		•	•	•	4				•		•	5.50	40	•	•	•	•	•		•	•
Nelthorpe Arms	Barton upon Humber	111		•	•	•	•				•		•	6	50	•	•	•	•	•		•	•
New Station Hotel	Lincoln	111		•			2	20	3		•		•	9	160	•	•	•	•	•		•	•
The Old Mill	Barton Upon Humber	111		•			3				•		•	5	50	•	•	•	•	•		•	•
The Old Plough Inn	Tuxford	111		•	•		3				•	•	•	9	40	•	•	•	•	•		•	•
Parkies	Scunthorpe	111												5	30	•	•	•	•	•			•
Planet Masala R.	Lincoln	111		•		•					•	•	•	7	144	•	•	•	•	•		•	•
The Plough Inn	Sleaford	112		•	•		2	50			•		•	7	50	•	•	•	•	•		•	•
Prince of Wales	Lincoln	112		•			5				•		•	4	30	•	•	•	•	•		•	•
Railway Hotel	Woodhall Spa	112		•	•		1	50	3		•		•	6	20	•	•	•	•	•	•	•	•
Ramblers Hotel	Mablethorpe	112		•				25	6		•		•	12	16	•	•	•	•	•	•	•	•
The Riverside Inn	Woodhall Spa	112	•	•	•		2				•	•	•	8.50	36	•	•	•	•	•	•	•	•
St Vincent Arms	Newark on Trent	112		•			2				•		•	6.50	60	•	•	•	•	•		•	•
Ship Inn	Sleaford	113		•	•	•	2				•		•	5	60	•	•	•	•	•		•	•
The Thatch	Brigg	113		•	•		1				•	•	•	6.50	80	•	•	•	•	•		•	•

102

Establishment	Nearest Town	Page No.	Waterside Setting	All Day Opening	Pets Welcome	Takeaway	Real Ales	Rooms From £	No. Bedrooms	Baby Changing	Child Portions	Play Area	Garden	Average Price	No. of Covers	Vegetarian Food	Credit Cards	Functions	Live Music	Coaches Welcome	Air Conditioning	No Smoking	Disabled Access
Victorian House R.	Grimsby	113			●					●	●			12	45	●	●	●	●		●	●	●
The Vines	Brigg	113		●							●			11	46	●	●	●	●		●		●
White Hart	Scunthorpe	113											●	4.50	75	●	●	●	●		●	●	●
White Hart Inn	Gainsborough	113					1	35	4				●		20	●	●	●	●		●		●
White Swan	Lincoln	114	●	●	●	●	4	20	4		●		●	6	50	●	●	●	●		●		●
White Swan H. (1)	Barton upon Humber	114	●	●	●	●	3	35	7		●	●	●	6	100	●	●	●	●	●	●	●	●
White Swan H. (2)	Bawtry	114	●		●	●	3	160	10			●	●		100	●	●	●		●	●		●
Winteringham F'lds	Barton upon Humber	114			●	●					●		●	38	48	●	●	●	●				
Yates Wine Lodge	Lincoln	114												5	20	●	●	●	●	●	●	●	
Ye Olde Whyte S.	Louth	114		●	●	●	3	25	7					5	50	●	●	●	●		●		●

Antimino's Ristorante
150 High Street
Scunthorpe

☎ 01724 276800
Location:

This family run restaurant specialises in steaks and fish yet still retains its range of quality pizzas and pasta dishes. Pop in for Italian coffee and biscuits, 'family time' between 5.30pm and 6.30pm for meal deals, for a romantic dinner or a get together with friends. Open until midnight with monthly live music.
At the top end of the High Street.

Ashby Star Inn
Rochdale Road
Ashby
Scunthorpe
☎ 01724 871117
Location:

A lovely, community pub that serves wholesome food such as battered haddock, vegetable lasagne and curries, and OAPs can eat 2 courses for just £2.99. Everyone loves the live music and discos, as well as 2 pool tables, a jukebox, large screen tv for all the sporting events, a new air hockey table plus a function room.
1/2 a mile from the town centre.

The Attic Bar
8A Park Street
Lincoln

☎ 01522 531722
Location:

This new venue offers great value food and drink and a host of entertainment. Authentic Thai dishes are served from 12-7pm, there's a good selection of wines and cocktails, and lagers start from just £2 a pint! Live music every Tuesday, DJs from Thursday to Saturday and a jamming session on Sundays.
Just off the High Street.

Balti House Restaurant
30 Alexander Road
Cleethorpes

☎ 01472 601359
Location:

This family run restaurant is open every day from 5pm, offering a unique opportunity to sample fantastic Indian food, free from artificial additives and colourings. With 25 years experience, Mr Iqubal Uddin can cook any dish on request, using only natural ingredients and fresh spices. 10% discount on takeaways.
On the seafront.

The Beach Bar
High Street
Sutton on Sea

☎ 01507 441453
Location: (EC P.221)

This friendly, community pub welcomes both locals and tourists and is now run by John Hanley who has refurbished to give a fresh look. He serves a good lunchtime menu, including fresh haddock & chips and juicy burgers. Children enjoy their own room and the patio and conservatory offer fantastic sea views.
Right on the seafront, at the edge of the town centre.

The Black Horse (1)
Chapel Lane
Nettleham

☎ 01522 750702
Location:

This old-fashioned pub serves traditional English food and 5 well kept real ales. Choose from dishes such as crusty pies and succulent steaks and a great roast lunch on Sundays. Idyllically set on the village green, let the folk and blues bands entertain you every month and try your skill in the pub quiz on Sundays.
Overlooking the village green.

The Black Horse (2)
31 South Street
Alford

☎ 01507 466853
Location:

It's nice to find a drinking only pub that is friendly and family orientated. Open all day, there's 1 real ale, which changes every week, and plenty of entertainment. Try karaoke on Fridays, dance at the Saturday discos, listen to live music or play pool and darts. Traditionally furnished and with a large car park.
Close to the market place.

Black Horse Chambers
6 Eastgate
Lincoln

☎ 01522 544404
Location:

Close to the cathedral and boasting old beams and a real fire, this is an idyllic, intimate setting in which to enjoy a fantastic dining experience. Both traditional and Continental cuisine is served, with delights such as Oriental mussels and lemon & raspberry panacotta. Now open 7 days a week for both lunch and dinner.
Close to the cathedral.

The Black Horse Inn
Mill Lane
Grainthorpe

☎ 01472 388229
Location:

The quiet location of this old English pub, with a real fire, makes it an ideal spot for a relaxing, peaceful drink in the extensive beer garden. Home cooked food too, served lunchtime and evening, such as lasagne, mixed grill and crusty pies. There are 4 guest ales and an improved wine list, pub games and a regular quiz.
By the green in the centre of the village.

The Carnival Inn
114 Tofts Road
Barton upon Humber

☎ 01652 634845
Location:

Under new and enthusiastic management, this traditional, drinking only pub is largely a music venue with high quality live bands every Friday. There's a music quiz on Mondays plus a pub games night every Wednesday. The large car park is ideal for coach parties and bikers, and all functions are welcomed.
A mile from the centre.

The Castle Hotel
& Knights Restaurant
Westgate
Lincoln
☎ 01522 538801
Location:

Owners, Mark and Diane Worrall have continued the tradition of outstanding food and high quality accommodation. Close to Lincoln Cathedral and Castle, there are 19 en suite guest rooms from £67 inclusive of breakfast, plus super evening meals on the delicious a la carte menu. An ideal venue for tourists.
In the city centre.

City Vaults
105 High Street
Lincoln

☎ 01522 521035
Location:

This modern and stylish pub is now managed by Morisa Gibb, who has introduced a fantastic new menu with delicious dishes like steak & onion baguettes, Shepherd's pie, Lincolnshire sausages and a roast of the day. There's good entertainment too with regular karaoke, singers, comics and theme nights.
Less than a mile from the centre.

105

Cromwells Restaurant
34 Market Place
Tattershall

☎ 01526 342300
Location: (EC P.219)

Within the Fortescue Arms, this delightful, new restaurant, run by Chef du Patron Mark Broadbent, offers a seasonally changing menu of delicious English food. Tempting, home-made desserts include blackberry cheesecake and Creme Brulée. Family friendly and all types of functions are welcomed. *On the market, within the Fortescue Arms.*

Cross Keys Inn
Main Street
Fulstow

☎ 01507 363223
Location:

This friendly, village pub is now run by Linda Mumby who serves a fantastic array of wholesome dishes, including specials of the week like pork spare ribs in barbecue sauce and chicken lasagne. Childrens portions are available and kids will appreciate the large, secure garden. Open all day on Saturday and Sunday. *Centrally located.*

Don Giovanni
18 Sincill Street
Lincoln

☎ 01522 534400
Location: (EC P.223)

A real feel of Italy, with authentic stone baked pizza, lasagne, wild mushroom pasta and a host of enticing Italian desserts, as well as pavement tables for alfresco dining in summer. On the first floor there are large windows and a balcony which afford delightful views of the historic streets of Lincoln. *Close to the railway and bus stations, near the city centre.*

Durham Ox
Main Road
Thimbleby

☎ 01507 526871
Location: (EC P.228)

A country pub on the edge of the village which has a real fire and a friendly ambience. Dean and Chrissie serve 2 good real ales and a nice selection of food such as home-made chilli, salmon in an orange and cream sauce and a mega mixed grill which is not for the faint hearted! Suitable for all types of private functions. *On the village outskirts on the B1190.*

Dynasty Chinese Rest.
10 Pavilion Row
Doncaster Road
Scunthorpe
☎ 01724 866662
Location:

New owners, the Yau family provide a warm welcome, excellent food and superb service. Open for lunch and dinner, 7 days a week, there are some fabulous dishes to sample. Try Chinese style fillet steak or the fabulous Oriental buffet, available Sunday to Thursday, where you can eat as much as you like. *1/2 a mile from the centre.*

Ebrington Arms
Main Street
Kirkby on Bain

☎ 01526 354560
Location:

A warm and friendly atmosphere has been created here by new owners Ronnie & Cathy. They serve 5 real ales, with a changing guest ale every week, and are commended by CAMRA. There's an extensive menu of traditional British food, from fresh salads to juicy steaks and a superb choice of home-made desserts. *In the village centre.*

Epernay Champagne & Seafood Restaurant
St Paul's Lane, Bailgate
Lincoln
☎ 01522 569284
Location: (EC P.218)

Unique in style, food and drink! A fantastic range of fresh seafood, including sea bass, lobster and scallops, plus many other tempting dishes like mushroom risotto and goats cheese with beetroot salad. Superb wine list and a wide selection of both well known and less familiar champagnes.
In the middle of the Bailgate area.

The Fairways Golf & Country Club
53 Sleaford Road
Tattershall
☎ 01526 344420
Location:

This truly English pub is set in large grounds and boasts a big beer garden and ample parking. Now with new management and catering staff, the service and the quality of food is fantastic. Eat in the bar or the a la carte restaurant and taste delights like Barnsley chops and roast duck in orange sauce. Kids welcome.
Next to Tattershall castle.

Fleece Inn
Lock Road
North Cotes

☎ 01472 388233
Location: (EC P.222)

Steven King has a hat trick of 'Gold Citations' from 'Lincolnshire Life' magazine from 2001 to 2003. A lovely olde worlde pub that dates back to 1845 and is festooned with historic photos of the village. With partner, Lianne, he runs this family venue, with superb pub food, good real ales and a good choice of pub games.
Right in the centre.

Food For Thought Coffee Shop
6 Rectory Lane
Branston
☎ 01522 797970
Location:

New owner, Jane Parkes has created a relaxed and friendly environment in which to meet friends, and provides both historical and modern information on the surrounding area. Her dishes are prepared using local produce, such as home-made soups, fresh salads, hot paninis and a lovely selection of cakes.
On the B1188, centrally located.

George & Dragon
High Street
Hagworthingham

☎ 01507 588255
Location: (EC P.221)

Jackie & Martin have made this into a fabulous, family orientated pub. The garden has a new adventure trail for children who also have their own menu. Food is served from 12-9pm, with home-made specials such as chicken & bacon pie and mild curry rice bake, plus a super Sunday carvery, great value at £6.95.
In the centre of the village on the A158.

The Glass House
Unit 9
St Mark's Square
Lincoln
☎ 01522 530871
Location:

Just a short walk from the city centre, this pub is lots of fun. The food is of a high standard and includes a full selection of superb international dishes, all of which are excellent value for money. From simple to the exotic, something to suit everyone. Good value drinks plus 30% discount on food for students.
A short walk from the town centre.

Directory

The Haywain
Motel & Free House
Ulceby Cross
Alford
☎ 01507 462786
Location: (EC P.214)

An ideal base for a trip to the coast or for visiting Lincoln and surrounding towns. 19 en suite rooms, with tvs and hot drink facilities, from just £32.50 per room. 2 real ales and super food from soups to honey roast duck and fruit pies. There's a separate function room too and a meeting room for businesses. *At the crossroads of the A16 & A1028.*

The Homestead
Canwick Avenue
Bracebridge Heath
Lincoln
☎ 01522 546400
Location: (EC P.228)

The best of both worlds here, the traditional feel of a pub, but with a restaurant atmosphere. New manager, Karen Dobbs has refurbished throughout and has successfully introduced live entertainment. Lovely food from English to Indian and Mexican. Outside you'll find a garden and patio as well as a play area. *2 miles south of Lincoln on the A15.*

Hope & Anchor
Sluice Road
South Ferriby

☎ 01652 635242
Location:

What a place! At the meeting point of 3 rivers, this traditional free house with a fine restaurant is everything you could ask for. Delicious cuisine, utilising local produce, is all freshly cooked and can be complemented by fine wines or 5 well kept real ales. Sip a glass of champagne and watch the glorious sunset. *On the A1077, 2 miles west of Barton.*

The Juice Bar Cafe
Total Fitness Health Club
Kingsly Road
Lincoln
☎ 01522 683222
Location:

Under the new ownership of Debbie & Julie, you'll find a huge improvement in the quality of food. You can enjoy fresh and healthy dishes, such as soups, salads and filled jacket potatoes, available to takeaway too, and a large selection of hot and cold drinks. Open to everyone, not just health club members. *Off the A46, in the Lincoln Fields Industrial Estate.*

Kind Bar & Restaurant
266 High Street
Lincoln

☎ 01522 530111
Location: (EC P.214)

This individually styled bar has a relaxing atmosphere with cool decor, leather sofas and air conditioning. Delicious food all day, with a seasonally changing menu of home-made dishes, plus a great Sunday roast. Good entertainment from open mic' nights and DJs to breakdancing. 10% discount on production of guide. *At the top of the hill facing down the High Street.*

Kings Arms
Main Street
Clarborough

☎ 01777 701246
Location: (EC P.217)

Chef du Patron, Ben Edwards has over 25 years experience so you can be assured of an outstanding dining experience here. He serves fresh, modern cuisine, with international influences such as Caribbean chicken. Delicious home-made desserts too. A warm and friendly atmosphere with a roaring fire in the winter. *In the village centre.*

Landings Hotel
& Restaurant
2-4 Cleethorpes Road
Grimsby
☎ 01472 342257
Location: **(EC P.223)**

This comfortable, 11 roomed hotel, with rates from £41.95 with breakfast, provides an eclectic mixture of food, with a choice of English, French and Chinese dishes. An international wine list, with English and European beers provides something for everyone. Look out for the spectacular garden and patio. *Just off the A180.*

The Lifeboat Bar
38 High Street
Cleethorpes

☎ 01472 320774
Location:

Completely refurbished, this venue now represents a modern, and trendy city bar, unique to Cleethorpes. Simple, tasty food, well presented, such as paninis, pastas, salads and tempting cheesy chips with bacon! Open from 10am for real coffees, with super entertainment from acoustic evenings to DJs at weekends. *Near both the centre and the seafront.*

The Lynton
Taylors Avenue
Cleethorpes

☎ 01472 691565
Location: **(EC P.217)**

Now run by Amanda & Phil Brierley, this traditional pub boasts a carvery restaurant where you can dine for as little as £3.45. There are also bar and a la carte menus, with delights such as Lincolnshire sausages, succulent steaks and fresh fish. Lots to do with pool, darts, Tuesday pub quiz and weekend entertainment. *A mile from the centre.*

Mariners Rest
Albert Street East
Grimsby

☎ 01472 353803
Location:

An exciting venue, now run by Shell & Steve Arliss who offer a week packed with entertainment, from karaoke and discos to great live music. The new menu features traditional English favourites and there are 2 real ales to sample too. Open all day, there's a friendly and welcoming atmosphere and great service. *Behind the Freeman Road Shopping Centre.*

The Market Hotel
West Carr Road
Ordsall

☎ 01777 703278
Location: **(EC P.220)**

Recognised for the quality of its real ales, this family owned, grade II listed free house has an astonishing 8 varieties to choose from. Wonderful food too, with succulent steaks and fresh fish and a good choice of daily specials. The Sunday carvery is not to be missed (booking advisable), nor is the monthly jazz night. *Near the railway station.*

Masons Arms
Spital Hill
Retford

☎ 01777 860760
Location:

Now run by Paul and Lisa, this traditional pub has been refurbished to provide a cosy and comfortable atmosphere. Open all day from 10.30am, the function room is ideal for all types of party and there's a large car park too. Karaoke every Friday and singers on Saturdays plus bar meals coming soon. *A few minutes walk from the town centre.*

Masons Arms Hotel
Cornmarket
Louth

☎ 01507 609525
Location: **(EC P.222)**

Under new and enthusuastic ownership, this grade II listed hotel dates back to 1725. There are 10 non-smoking bedrooms, which start from £30 including a super breakfast, and a fantastic a la carte menu featuring seasonal specialities like dressed crab and crayfish tails. Commended by CAMRA and dog friendly too. *In the town centre.*

The Mayflower
Margaret Street
Immingham

☎ 01469 577542
Location:

New manager, Suzanne Best has introduced a fantastic bar menu of delicious dishes such as giant Yorkshire puddings with various fillings, hot chilli and succulent steaks. On Wednesday you can have 2 main meals for just £5.50 or 2 courses for only £4.50. Pub games, live music, Thursday quiz and karaoke on Fridays. *1/2 a mile from the town centre.*

Mermaid Inn
Seaholme Road
Mablethorpe

☎ 01507 473321
Location:

This delightful free house offers something completely different for Mablethorpe. Super food, from fresh baguettes, jacket potatoes and juicy burgers to steak, gammon and chicken sizzlers. Children appreciate their own room and there's plenty to do with pub games, quiz nights and weekend entertainment. *Set on the edge of the caravan site.*

Mill House Elms Hotel
London Road
Retford

☎ 01777 708957
Location:

Open all day, the Mill House Elms Hotel is renowned locally for its food, with fish & chips in beer batter a firm favourite and its real ales which include Pedigree and Bass. Just 1 mile from the pretty market town of Retford, with 19 en suite and disabled rooms (prior notice required). Excellent function facilities too. *On the A638, south of the town centre.*

My Father's Moustache
North Holme Road
Louth

☎ 01507 607796
Location: **(EC P.224)**

Stephen and Melanie have made many improvements to this unusually named pub. There's a bar menu served in the large restaurant area, where you can choose from a range of home-made, English dishes and several daily specials. Good real ales and a superb function room. Winners of 'Best Kept Frontage'. *1/4 mile from the north exit of the A16 into Louth.*

The Nags Head
1 Thornton Road
Wootton

☎ 01469 588253
Location: **(EC P.224)**

Voted 'Inspired Pub of the Year 2004' and run by Maureen and Paul Woods who offer a friendly welcome to the whole family. They serve a menu of traditional, wholesome dishes such as battered haddock & chips plus a fantastic 2 course lunch for £3.50 Monday to Friday. Tuesday quiz and 4 real ales. *On the edge of the village, on the A1077.*

Nelthorpe Arms
School Lane
South Ferriby

☎ 01652 635235
Location: (EC P.216)

This C17th pub has been beautifully refurbished by Gavin Richards to include 3 en suite rooms. He serves a lovely, home-made menu, utilising local produce, like pork in a creamy apple sauce, and caters for all functions. Live music, karaoke, a quiz on Wednesday and chilli nights the last Thursday in the month. *In the heart of the village, which is 2 miles west of Barton.*

The New Station Hotel
Station Road
Langworth

☎ 01522 750475
Location: (EC P.225)

This lovely free house has become more of a 'gastro' pub, yet has retained its wonderful character. Under new ownership, it is now open every day and the choice of food is tremendous. Try the home-made steak & kidney pie or vegetarian fajitas followed by tempting cheesecake or indulgent chocolate fudge cake. *By the railway crossing on the A158.*

The Old Mill
Kings Garth Mill
Market Lane
Barton-upon-Humber
☎ 01652 660333
Location:

Dating to 1803, built on the site of a Norman castle, this former chalk mill is adorned with historic pictures. Fabulous food, with dishes like chicken & mushroom pie, freshly battered Grimsby haddock and a super roast on Sundays. Well kept ales, a nice choice of wines and Italian coffees and live music on Thursdays. *Just off the Market Place.*

The Old Plough Inn
Main Street
Egmanton

☎ 01777 872565
Location: (EC P.225)

Now run by Mark and Matt, who are both qualified chefs so you can expect a high calibre of food here. They have added an upstairs dining area, which is non-smoking, and serve a lovely menu from mussels to calves liver with smoked bacon, and a selection of fine desserts too. Food available all day. *In the centre of the village.*

Parkies
84 Mary Street
Scunthorpe

☎ 01724 844382
Location:

Now under new tenancy, this town pub has vastly improved and offers a safe and friendly atmosphere. A new bar menu is served from 12-4pm with food like filled jacket potatoes and juicy burgers & chips and there's a full Sunday lunch. Disco Friday and Saturday, monthly karaoke, pool and table football. *On the edge of the town centre.*

Planet Masala
Odeon Complex, Unit 4
Brayford Wharf North
Lincoln
☎ 01522 511511
Location: (EC P.219)

'May the spice be with you!' Open from 11am every day, this Indian themed restaurant offers food from around the world. Try Indian curries, Indian pizzas and Mexican grills, to name a few. The daily buffet is great value, available from 12-3pm, where you can eat as much as you like for just £5.99. Takeaway too. *Part of the Odeon Complex, beside the river.*

111

The Plough Inn
High Street
Walcott

☎ 01526 869015
Location: (EC P.216)

This very cosy free house keeps 3 real ales including a weekly guest. Martin & Irene Samuels serve an outstanding array of both traditional and a la carte cuisine, such as Grimsby haddock and succulent steaks. The pleasant atmosphere and the beautiful garden make this a nice place that will suit the whole family. *In the centre of the village.*

The Prince of Wales Inn
77A Bailgate
Lincoln

☎ 01522 528894
Location:

Open all day, landlady Jane Vasey serves a cracking choice of 5 real ales and a super range of food. Everything is home-made, from warming soups to crusty pies and homely casseroles, plus a lovely Sunday lunch. Just a 3 minute walk from Lincoln Cathedral, you can enjoy Sky tv, darts and an internet jukebox. *A short walk from the cathedral.*

Railway Hotel
Kirkstead Bridge
Kirkstead

☎ 01526 352580
Location:

Neil, Pauline & family have gradually improved the quality of this friendly hotel and now boast 3 redecorated en suite guest rooms. They serve delicious, home-made English food in the conservatory dining room and the function room is ideal for all parties. In winter, enjoy well kept ale in front of the roaring fire. *On the B1191, a mile west of Woodhall Spa.*

Ramblers Hotel
Sutton Road
Trusthorpe

☎ 01507 441171
Location:

This friendly and comfortable hotel is set in a quiet and relaxing location, yet is just 5 minutes walk from the seafront and 1 mile from Mablethorpe. Terry & Kim Lord have 6 guest rooms and offer a delicious choice of breakfasts, as well as an optional evening meal of freshly cooked English food. Fully licenced too. *On the coast road in the centre of the village.*

The Riverside Inn
Ferry Road
Southrey

☎ 01526 398374
Location:

Terry & Jennifer Browne, the new owners of this traditional free house, that dates back to 1896, are proud of the warm welcome they provide. They serve a delicious menu of home-made dishes, prepared from fresh, local produce, such as rabbit pie, succulent lamb shank, juicy steaks and a wonderful Sunday roast. *Just off the B119, east of Lincoln.*

St Vincent Arms
Main Street
Norton Disney

☎ 01522 788478
Location: (EC P.218)

This C17th, village pub is now run by Robin Stark who serves fine, traditional English food and some Mediterranean dishes, having spent several years in Portugal. Try classic chicken Piri Piri, wholesome casseroles and fresh sardines, all at great prices. Enjoy entertainment on Sundays with vocalists and comedians. *Just off the A6, in the centre of the village.*

The Ship Inn
20 High Street
Billinghay

☎ 01526 860756
Lcation: (EC P.226)

Refurbished throughout, this traditional village pub is now run by Phil and Ruth. They serve delicious English food in the restaurant such as scampi, mixed grills and succulent steaks as well as a fantastic carvery on Sundays. The function room is ideal for parties with its own bar, dance floor and DJ booth. *Off the A153, centrally located.*

The Thatch
High Street
Broughton

☎ 01652 655565
Location:

Now fully refurbished and run by David & Andrea who serve a tasty menu of home-made dishes such as steak & kidney pie, fresh fish and mixed grills. There are a selection of daily specials and Paninis, plus a range of tempting desserts, all of which can be savoured in the separate non-smoking restaurant. *In the middle of the village.*

Victorian House Restaurant
143 Welholme Road
Grimsby
☎ 01472 355832
Location:

An ideal restaurant for a special occasion where the quality of food is outstanding. Now open every day, fresh produce is brought in daily to create delights such as lobster Thermidore and fillet steak in Stilton sauce. Beautifully refurbished by new owner, Colleen Hyde who can meet any special requests. *3/4 of a mile from the centre.*

The Vines Café Bar & Restaurant
Wrawby Street
Brigg
☎ 01652 653174
Location: (EC P.220)

3 venues in 1 here, with a cosy bar, and a day time café which turns in to a delightful restaurant in the evening. New owners, George & Gillian Newcombe offer high quality cuisine, prepared from local produce, in an informal atmosphere. Try warm monkfish salad, liver & onions or pan fried tuna steaks. Superb! *On the edge of the town centre.*

The White Hart
96 High Street
Crowle

☎ 01724 710333
Location:

The oldest pub in the Isle of Axholme, dating to the C16th. A broad choice of quality food, like haddock in beer batter and steak & mushroom pie. Owner, Trevor Coles welcomes all the family to his olde worlde pub which has been refurbished, without losing its period charm. Good food and great ambience. *4 miles north of Junction 2 M180.*

White Hart Inn
Main Street
West Stockwith
Nr Gainsborough
☎ 01427 890176
Location: (EC P.227)

A lovely setting for this charming free house, at the intersection of the rivers Trent and Idle. Family owned and family welcoming, and beautifully refurbished, there is a wide range of food from a la carte to bar snacks and a lovely Sunday lunch. A pretty patio garden and en suite rooms are now available. *10 miles south of junction 2, off the M180.*

113

White Swan
Newark Road
Torksey Lock

☎ 01427 718653
Location: (EC P.226)

Next to the River Trent and the Fossdyke canal, this is an ideal venue for boaters and walkers. Enjoy a wide choice of home-made food, prepared by qualified chefs, from delicious starters through to tempting desserts and liqueur coffees, all served in the Cygnet Restaurant. Play area, weekly quiz and a roaring fire. *Beside the river, near the village centre.*

White Swan Hotel (1)
66 Fleetgate
Barton-upon-Humber

☎ 01652 632459
Location:

Now under new ownership, this grade II listed building boasts 4 guest bedrooms from only £20 pp, including a Continental breakfast. Completely refurbished, there's now a traditional bar and a 1970s theme bar, complete with old booths, staff in costume and a 1970s jukebox plus popular discos twice a week. *500 yards from the centre.*

White Swan Hotel (2)
Eel Pool Road
Drakeholes
Bawtry, Nr Doncaster
☎ 01777 817206
Location: (EC P.227)

Phil and Carol Smith are proud of their picturesque location, beside the Chesterfield canal, and the quality of their English food, created by 3 highly skilled chefs. They keep well conditioned cask ales and a fine selection of international wines. 7 of the bedrooms are en suite and from £35 are very good value. *Just off the A631, 4 miles east of Bawtry.*

Winteringham Fields Restaurant
Silver Street
Winteringham
☎ 01724 733096
Location: (EC P.215)

What a venue! Boasting 2 Michelin stars and 5 AA rosettes, this homely, yet luxurious restaurant serves the best of Modern British and French cuisine. Attention to detail is evident, a greeting in the car park, wonderful presentation and clarity of colour and taste with all dishes prepared from local produce. *In the centre of the village.*

Yates
274-277 High Street
Lincoln

☎ 01522 589478
Location:

A modern restaurant, that welcomes families during the day, and a popular bar, with relaxing sofas, that has extended opening at weekends. The interesting menu changes seasonally, and includes a Thursday curry night where you can choose a curry and a drink for just £4. Nice beer garden and a DJ on Saturdays. *At the top of the hill.*

Ye Olde Whyte Swanne
45 Eastgate
Louth

☎ 01507 601312
Location:

The pub, as the name suggests, has history dating back to 1612. Whilst the beams and fires are old, there are plenty of new ideas from new landlord Darren Cousins. 3 real ales and an English menu featuring a fantastic selection of home-made pies such as steak & Stilton and chicken & mushroom. 7 guest rooms too. *In the centre.*

114

Bengal Palace

11 Queen Street, Colchester. Tel: 01206 545045

An extensive menu of fine Indian cuisine, including our speciality salmon and lobster dishes.

Genuine Indian beers.

Takeaway available.

"An elegant restaurant where you can confidently leave yourself in the hands of very experienced and capable staff."

Red Rose Inn

The Street, Lindsey. Tel: 01449 741424

Good home cooked food, with some too tempting desserts! Good wines and ales and an inside & outside play area for children

"A grade II listed, fifteenth century coaching inn with bags of character. Beams and an inglenook fireplace create an atmospheric environment for all the family."

115

"Peter Webb has made dramatic improvements to this friendly local. A family orientated venue located just out of town and well worth a visit."

"This former smugglers' haunt dates back to 1358. It's a cosy inn and restaurant with an interesting old English menu and comfortable bedrooms."

116

The Cork Bar
Undercliff Road West, Felixstowe. Tel: 01394 283562

Our non-smoking restaurant serves excellent English dishes from fish & chips, to succulent steaks.

"Named after the Corksand Light Ship, this venue now boasts a beautiful new restaurant and has balconies overlooking the sea; just perfect for those balmy summer nights."

The Trafalgar
616 Main Road, Dovercourt. Tel: 01255 502234

Good value bar snacks served from 12-9pm, complemented by fine real ales. Themed evenings as well as regular live entertainment.

"Kevin & Justina now run this family orientated pub and host a variety of superb live entertainment events. The summer barbecues in the large beer garden are very popular."

117

The Brewery Tap

Cliff Quay, Ipswich. Tel: 01473 281508

We serve a varied, traditional menu and pride ourselves on the freshness of our ingredients. Excellent real ales and a broad international wine list.

FUNCTIONS WELCOMED

"A fine grade II listed venue overlooking the River Orwell, now expertly run by Angie Halsey. Lots of interesting Tolly Brewery memorabilia."

The Old Queen's Head

Ford Street, Aldham. Tel: 01206 241584

Our lunchtime a la carte menu specialises in fresh fish and unique vegetarian creations. Enquire about our themed evenings and 'jamming nights'.

"Julia Spence has created a lovely ambience at this delightful seventeenth century listed pub. Lots of innovative creations to savour from her very talented chef."

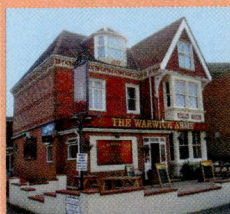

"Now returned to its original name and under new ownership, this family orientated venue has been refurbished and now boasts an elegant restaurant."

"A fourteenth century inn that's steeped in history and boasts a host of memorabilia. Family run and very family friendly; the children will love the aviary."

The Fox & Hounds

Church Street, Groton. Tel: 01787 210474

Our intersting menu is changed regularly and is all home-made, including our popular Sunday roast. Fine wines, excellent real ales and an even better welcome!

"Now run by Mary Fitzgerald, this olde worlde pub boasts lovely views over open countryside. There's a pretty beer garden, home to new petanque and boules pitches."

The Bull Inn

High Street, Cavendish. Tel: 01787 280245

Our charming pub has a real fire, old beams and simply oozes history! Quality real ales, good food and a pleasant beer garden.

"Now run by Paul & Lynn, this village pub is full of character and boasts a mouthwatering selection of English dishes with a modern twist, all freshly prepared by the highly skilled chef."

120

"Beautifully refurbished by Jon & Matthew Tindall, this is one of Ipswich's premier restaurants. Superb, modern cuisine, excellent wines and outstanding service."

"A beautifully designed, modern restaurant that specialises in Mediterranean cuisine. The Tropical Patio is a real oasis in the heart of Colchester!"

Penny's Bar & Restaurant

10-12 St Nicholas Street, Ipswich. Tel: 01473 280433

We give you the best of both worlds; outstanding, traditional Spanish tapas and a selection of fine English cuisine. Our upstairs function room is ideal for all types of parties.

"This listed building, complete with old beams, houses a wonderful Spanish bar and restaurant. Both Spanish and English food is available all day, as well as Spanish beers and of course Sangria. You can also have a go at Salsa dancing!"

Honeymoon Chinese Restaurant

7 Old Pier Street, Walton-on-the-Naze. Tel: 01255 670888

Don't miss the Sunday buffet! Eat as much as you like for a very reasonable price. Experiment with spectacular Cantonese, Peking & Thai dishes.

"A true Oriental welcome greets you on entering this delightful seaside venue. Beautifully presented food in a clean and fresh environment."

122

"Set in 5 acres of pretty countryside, this delightful, grade II listed, seventeenth century free house has been lovingly restored by Neil & Gillian Mason. Close to Southwold and many attractions, this is the perfect base for exploring the region"

"Set amidst the beautiful waterside location of Snape Maltings, The Plough & Sail offers an innovative, Modern English menu in a light, fresh dining room. Perfect for all the family."

124

"A delightful pub that is a fine example of a village local. Now run by Lynn & Alan Bailey who have created a fine menu of old English country cooking."

"A modern and stylish restaurant with beautifully etched glass partitions creating a convivial atmosphere in which to enjoy sumptuous cuisine, coupled with efficient and friendly service."

125

THE ⬤ DOG ....AT GRUNDISBURGH

The Green, Grundisburgh. Tel: 01473 735267

Our eighteenth century pub boasts two open fires and is full of antique and period furniture. Our food is unashamedly traditional English, but with a modern twist! We have excellent real ales and an interesting wine list where we source superb wines from small vineyards.

"Run by James & Charles Rogers, The Dog has great diversity with something for everyone. Excellent ales, well sourced and unusual wines and superb food. Try the roast organic salmon with a sweet chilli & ginger dressing."

126

"An award winning Chef du Patron is the new owner of this contemporary Indian restaurant, on the edge of the town centre. Superb, fast & efficient service and very good disabled facilities."

"Formerly 'The Black Boy', an eighteenth century cockfighting venue, this spacious olde worlde pub is in the heart of Witham. Suitable for famiies, with good ales, food and an atmosphere to match!"

127

"After twenty-seven years experience in this industry, Derek Williams has settled at this friendly local. He has made a host of improvements and has recently re-introduced food."

"Renowned for the excellence of both its food and service, this venue is frequented by 'the great and the good', including many local MPs."

128

"This former drovers' and coaching inn, dates back to the fifteenth century and exhibits much interesting memorabilia. Tastefully refurbished by new owners Graham and Jackie."

"A thirteenth century, former smugglers' inn with legends of secret tunnels to the church and the nearby Abbey Castle. A real sense of history at this rustic venue; the accommodation is excellent."

"A superb venue for all those who love consistently high quality, freshly fried fish & chips. Enquire about the children's party service too."

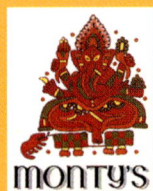

"Owned by the Chhetri family, who have been involved with restaurants for over 26 years! This 400 year old, listed building is tastefully furnished and features many antiques."

130

"Originally a brewery, this 400 year old establishment is now run by Chris White who has already won numerous awards. The setting is just lovely."

"Lucille Moran, a former manager and now tenant, runs this lively, sporty venue that is host to a wide variety of entertainment that will suit all ages."

131

"A family owned restaurant with a fantastic family atmosphere, outstanding service and a host of culinary delights. Don't miss the annual 'Charity Day'."

"This seventeenth century pub is now run by Lisa & Darren who have created a family friendly atmosphere. Ideally located on the A140, this is a great stopoff point for a lovely meal and to let the kids have a run!".

132

Graham's on the Green

12-14 The Green, Writtle. Tel: 01245 422432.

We serve a fantastic menu of Modern European cuisine. Dine in one of our intimate alcoves or on the cosy heated patio. Regular themed evening menus & light jazz on Tuesdays.

"A fabulous new, elegant restaurant with all the style of 'The West End', but with a country view over the village green, complete with pond!"

133

The Ship

The Street, South Walsham. Tel: 01603 270049

We serve a full menu of traditional English fayre, with 'Winter Warmer' offers and a 'Curry Night' on Wednesdays. We welcome the whole family.

"A friendly village local, run by Giles & Kim Naylor that is full of character. The snug has a cosy open fire and there is a separate function room for hire."

Lucky Star Chinese Restaurant

7 – 8 Pier Terrace, Lowestoft, NR33 0AB

TEL: 01502 573 397

We serve authentic and traditional Chinese dishes and beverages with a range of superb House Specialities.

"A fabulous new restaurant owned by Jenny & Michael (Chef Du Patron). He has many years of experience in London's 'China Town', so you can be assured of true Chinese food."

134

Ye Olde Buck Inn
29, The Street, Honingham. Tel: 01603 880393

Traditional a la carte and bar menus, with varied Daily Specials and a cracking Sunday lunch! Enjoy our lovely beer garden and there's a marquee for functions up to 120.

"A delightful thatched inn dating back to the 1600s and named after smuggler John Buck. Fantastic character enhanced by 2 friendly ghosts!"

The Robert Kett
Lime Tree Avenue, Wymondham. Tel: 01953 602957

Try our traditional country cooking at both lunchtime and in the evening. Our 4 real ales are in excellent condition and we have monthly live music.

"Named after its local hero, and sister to 'Ye Olde Buck Inn', this establishment is very family orientated and is excellent value for money with very large portions."

The Royal Oak

High Street, Laxfield. Tel: 01986 798446

Come and sample our
excellent new menu in our
non-smoking restaurant.
'Senior Citizen 2 course
specials' on Wednesdays.

FAMILIES WELCOME   SEPARATE GAMES ROOM

"An olde worlde village pub, full of character, now run by Martin & Sharon Handley. They have completely refurbished and introduced an exciting new menu."

The Black Swan

25 Norwich Road, Horsham St. Faith, Norwich. Tel: 01603 8977878

The highlight of our
delicious home-made dishes
is our Sunday roast. Both
families and functions are
welcomed and watch out for
our monthly live
entertainment.

"This historic venue has a host of famous customers, most notably King Charles II and fighter pilot ace Douglas Bader. Now fully refurbished, with an elegant restaurant."

136

"Everything is authentic, from the elegant decor and beautiful Thai carvings to the sumptuous food and interesting local wines and beers."

"An award winning establishment, commended by both CAMRA and the 'Norwich Evening News'. Now run by Richard & Michaela who put on several beer festivals throughout the year."

137

"Roz & Ronny have been very busy refurbishing and have converted the barn to a self-contained, comfortable letting room, as well as creating an exciting adventure playground for children."

"Set within 3 acres of wonderful display gardens, enjoy an 'out of town dining experience.' Awarded 5 stars by the 'Eastern Daily Press'."

138

"A seventeenth century, historic building, with a beautifully refurbished function room. All caravanners will welcome the adjacent five pitch site with electric hook-up."

"A delightful, grade II listed, sixteenth century hotel, now fully refurbished and boasting a lovely conservatory and a relaxing lounge area."

The Crawfish Inn

Holt Road, Thursford. Tel: 01328 878313

Choose from our superb selection of Thai dishes, which feature many vegetarian options.

"Wonderful Thai cuisine utilising traditional fresh herbs and spices. Everything is prepared with the ultimate care and precision."

The Restaurant At Hermanus

Hermanus Leisure Centre, The Holway, Winterton-on-Sea.
Tel: 01493 393607

We serve a varied menu of tempting dishes on both our bar and restaurant menus, with fresh fish a popular feature. Three function rooms available and there's regular entertainment.

"Now owned by Vaughan Cutter & Glen Bowles. The Hermanus is set in an idyllic and unspoilt fishing village, this is a perfect base from which to explore the delightful Norfolk coastline. Convenient for both Great Yarmouth and Norwich."

140

The Railway Tavern

Station Road, Coltishall. Tel: 01603 738316

Real home-made food, featuring daily specials. CAMRA recognised real ales and live entertainment. What more could you want?

"A charming, seventeenth century free house, now owned by Sam & Ro, set in 2 acres of grounds. A host of outdoor events in summer, including a beer festival."

The Crown Hotel

25 High Street, Watton. Tel: 01953 882375

Perfect for business or pleasure, with traditional English food served lunchtimes and evenings. Function facilities to suit all occasions.

"This historic, eighteenth century coaching inn is set in the heart of the town and has been refurbished throughout, by owners Shirley and Hayley, now providing comfortable accommodation."

141

"This unique restaurant brings both the taste & theatre of Japan to East Anglia. Excellent food cooked in front of you with a theatrical flourish!"

"A picturesque inn dating to 1610 that retains many original features, including 2 open fires. Amongst Alister Dwelly's many improvements is the new menu!"

142

143

The Hog in Armour
16 Charing Cross, Norwich. Tel: 01603 660355

You are assured of the highest standards with all our food created by Master Chef of Great Britain, Kevin Gardner. Our 2 beautifully decorated function rooms are available for both business and social parties.

"Now run by the excellent chef, Kevin Gardner who has finished a beautiful restoration, creating a spacious, airy, yet cosy environment. The food is something special."

The Falcon Inn
The Green, Pulham Market. Tel: 01379 676268

Try the many exciting dishes on our brand new menu, all of which are freshly prepared by our highly skilled chef.

WE WELCOME THE WHOLE FAMILY

"Positioned in a pretty position overlooking the village green, this archetypal country local is now owned by Michael & Beverley Smith, who boast an elegant restaurant and a new indoor play area."

144

"New owner, Anne Bishop has refreshed everything, from the decor to the menus. A very friendly environment with lovely sea views."

"A beautifully refurbished restaurant under the new ownership of Rachael & Jeremy Parke. They serve a changing menu of modern dishes utilising local organic and free-range produce."

146

The Angel

Lower Olland Street, Bungay. Tel: 01986 892507

Sample our wonderful traditional English food as well as the Sunday carvery which is simply the best, and at just £5.95, fantastic value. Rooms available from just £30.

"Set in the middle of Bungay, this quaint and very historic pub dating back to 1518, has beams aplenty and even secret tunnels! Good food and excellent value rooms."

Duke of York

8 Norwich Road, Ditchingham. Tel: 01986 895558

We serve wholesome English fayre as well as simply gorgeous desserts and ice-creams. Beer drinkers will love our lovingly kept Adnams!

"Now owned by Tina & Ian, this is a good venue for a family meal as well as real ale enthusiasts. The secure beer garden is perfect for children of all ages."

147

148

"Stone floors, wooden settles, open fires and superb food created by an AA Rosette holder. Try 'Nelson's Blood', a secret recipe of rum and mixed spice!"

"A well established, award winning takeaway, that now boasts a new restaurant. Enjoy watching the chefs at work by viewing through the open kitchen."

149

"David Archer is the proud winner of Le Routiers award for hospitality, first class service and ambience. A riverside free house with stunning views and its very own ferry!"

150

"This award winning restaurant is owned by Siraprapha Mitchell. All the highly skilled chefs are recruited from the top hotels in Thailand."

"An atmospheric pub with a delightful covered courtyard that is close to the National Cycle Route and a short walk from the river."

151

The White Hart
The Thoroughfare, Halesworth. Tel: 01986 873386

We serve delicious restaurant and bar menus, as well as daily specials seven days a week and a full Sunday lunch. Children are welcome and we have a pleasant patio and garden.
REAL ALES & FINE WINES

" Now under the tenancy of Phil Tompkins, this wonderful, grade II listed building, set in the historic town of Halesworth, has an atmospheric interior, festooned with old photographs."

The Red Lion
Church Street, Coltishall. Tel: 01603 737402

We serve an a la carte menu in the evenings and an extensive bar menu all day. Three real ales & a range of good wines. Our popular Family Room has a soft play area.

"Owners Peter & Melanie have put great emphasis on being family friendly at their historic, seventeenth century venue. The interior soft play area is fantastic for young children."

152

The Ostrich Inn

**Fakenham Road, South Creake, Nr Fakenham
Tel: 01328 82332**

We serve delicious home-made food, with many old favourites. Treat yourself to lobster, chips & a glass of bubbly! Indulge yourself and then stay in one of our fabulous en suite rooms.

NEW COCKTAIL MENU

"A delightful, grade II listed free house, now owned by Simon & Emma, who have completely refurbished, creating a rustic barn restaurant and a pretty courtyard. This is one ostrich that definitely hasn't got its head buried in the sand!"

The White Horse

The Street, Corton. Tel: 01502 730294

Enjoy our wonderful, freshly cooked food in either the bar, restaurant or our airy conservatory. We serve a fine range of wines and good English real ales. Our summer barbecues are a huge success.

"A pleasant coastal venue, now run by Andy and Natalie, who have created a family orientated venue."

153

"A well established venue on the outskirts of the university town of Cambridge, now run by Amanda & Philip Wharrier. Superb en suite accommodation as well as a pretty, heated patio."

"One of the newest restaurants in this historic city, with modern decor and a friendly atmosphere. Enjoy fast and efficient service, as well as a host of new house specialities."

155

Hat & Feathers

35 Barton Road, Cambridge. Tel: 01223 350723

Our heated courtyard is a wonderful year round facility, where you can enjoy a varied bar menu , real ales and a good wine list. Watch out for our monthly live entertainment.

"A traditional family pub just a short walk from the city centre. Expertly managed by Sean McGuirk who has introduced a delicious new menu."

White Horse

Rede Road, Whepstead. Tel: 01284 735542

Enjoy freshly cooked food at our traditional and historic, C17th, country pub, as well as a selection of wines and 3 real ales.

"This delightful venue is now under new management. Bags of character, with low beams and a real fire, as well as a pretty garden, makes this an ideal family hostelry."

156

"A delightful village inn, now owned by Alfred & Esther, just outside Cambridge. The 4 rooms provide an ideal base from which to explore this beautiful and historic city."

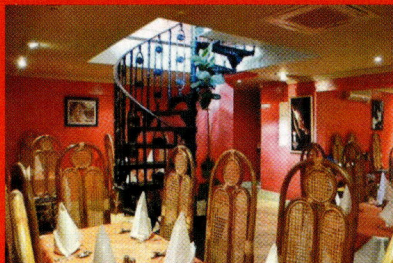

"Close to both the city centre and train station, this new concept offers a modern and minimalist environment, coupled with friendly and efficient staff."

157

"This former bakery dates back to the 1500s and retains bags of character with beams aplenty and open fires. Great improvements by new owners Simon & Mary Barker."

"This thirteenth century, delightful venue is now run by Malcolm & Jo-Anne, who have tastefully refurbished to create a warm ambience where families are welcome."

"One of Cambridge's most historic venues. A pavilion named after the famous cricketer who once played on the beautiful setting you can observe from your table."

"This two level, Tudor pub, now run by John & Allyson Rogers simply oozes character. The garden is superb and is the venue for summer barbecues and hog roasts."

The Three Kings Inn

The Kings Lodge, Hengrave Road, Fornham All Saints. Tel: 01284 766979

Elegant en suite rooms with tv and internet connection. Fine wines and real ales and very family friendly!

We serve a nice range of traditional English fayre, utilising locally sourced produce.

" A delightful old coaching inn now run by Stuart & Karen. The stylish, well equipped en suite rooms have a 4 diamond rating and make an ideal base from which to explore the surrounding area."

The Cherry Tree

8 Duck Lane, Haddenham. Tel: 01353 740667

Come and see our new restaurant open Monday to Friday at lunchtimes and evenings and all day at the weekend. Our pretty beer garden is the venue for regular summer barbecues.

"A lovely country pub that serves freshly prepared, traditional English food and plays hosts to an annual beer festival that is not to be missed!"

160

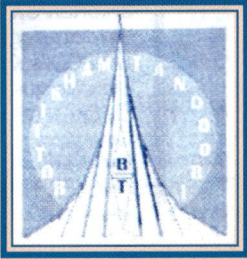

BOTTISHAM BRASSERIE

**4 High Street, Bottisham, Nr. Cambridge.
Telephone: 01223 813900**

Indian and Bangladeshi cuisine.

House specialities.

Open 7 days a week.

Fully licenced.

"Situated in the heart of this pleasant Cambridgeshire village, offering pleasant and authentic surroundings and an informal and relaxed dining atmosphere. Choose one of the varied and imaginative house specials."

161

162

163

The Swan Inn

Thetford Road, Coney Weston. Tel: 01359 221295

We specialise in good real ales, lovely fresh food, cooked to order and provide a warm, cosy atmosphere enhanced by real fires.

EXCELLENT FOLK MUSIC EVERY MONTH

"A family run pub that is at the very heart of this community. Kevin & Jean welcome the whole family and even entertain the kids whilst you enjoy a relaxing drink and a tasty bar snack."

The Lodge

29 High Street, Feltwell. Tel: 01842 828474

Enjoy real Mexican cuisine - Enchiladas, Tacos and much more, washed down with San Miguel beer in our comfortable dining room.

"Now run by Janet Jackson who has already made vast improvements. The Lodge is now impeccably clean with a warm atmosphere and a large and diverse menu."

165

The Chequers

36 Hill Street, Feltwell. Tel: 01842 827312

True home cooking with roast dinners every day of the week, or for something more exotic why not try wild boar or crocodile!

EXCELLENT ENTERTAINMENT AT WEEKENDS

"Jackie Sharpe has introduced an innovative new menu of home cooked dishes which can be enjoyed in the intimate, non-smoking conservatory restaurant."

The White Horse

Longstanton Road, Oakington. Tel: 01223 232417

We specialise in delicious, freshly prepared Mexican food, with a wide choice of daily specials. Full Sunday lunch served 12-6pm. All families very welcome.

"New tenants, Karen & Tony Collins have lovingly refurbished throughout and have created a beautiful beer garden where you can relax on those warm summer evenings, while the children play in the secure play area."

166

167

168

"Close to The Wash, this friendly and family orientated venue is now run by Tim & Sandie. They have introduced a new menu including some unusual ice-creams."

"Expertly managed by Simon Miles, this intimate restaurant has been beautifully restored. Experience a real taste of France and utilise the excellent function room for family occasions and business meetings."

The Greengage Hungry Horse

Tollgate Lane, Bury St. Edmunds. Tel: 01284 760796

We serve an all day menu that is excellent value for money. Our portions will feed the 'hungriest horse'! We have our own children's club and menu.

REGULAR ENTERTAINMENT

"Now expertly managed by the experienced Doug & Anita. They have introduced many improvements and have created a warm family atmosphere."

The Bushel Inn

Market Street, The Rookery, Newmarket. Tel: 01638 661727

We have a good old-fashioned, family run pub, serve 2 real ales and wholesome English food, as well as a full Sunday lunch.

"Tina, Eamon and their family have produced a really welcoming atmosphere in their newly refurbished town pub. Enjoy lovely home-made fayre including filling stews and warming soups."

The Black Horse

63 Orchard Road, Melbourn. Tel: 01763 226046

We are truly family orientated and offer a nice kids play area and summer barbecues for everyone. We serve good English food and have lots of entertainment!

"This pretty village pub is set in the heart of Melbourn. Bryan & Renee Walker welcome everyone and produce delicious home-made food; try the Norfolk steak pie, game and fresh fish."

171

The Royal Oak

Ixworth Thorpe. Tel: 01359 269740

We serve excellent home-made food at our archetypal country pub. Great value too, with lunch for 2 from £8. There's a cosy bar area and pub games too.

"Berenice serves an interesting menu in her non-smoking dining room. Seafood Mornay, Manor pie and Funky Banana cheesecake are just a few of the favourites. The kids play area is superb."

The Angel

41 School Road, Watlington. Tel: 01553 811326

Lots going on with good food, barbecues, OAP specials, hog roasts, live music, discos and theme nights too!

"Now run by new owners, Peter & Mandy, who provide a host of activities and are building a new children's play area. Nice food, try the Cajun chicken or baked trout, both are excellent!"

The Ickleton Lion

Abbey Street, Ickleton. Tel: 01799 530269

Come and enjoy the atmosphere of an English country pub in a lovely village. New Steak Nights where you can sample varieties such as steak Diane or steak in peppercorn sauce.

"Chris & Mirela have made great improvements at this delightful country venue. Lovely open fires, an excellent new menu and a pretty beer garden for summer are just a few of the delights that await you."

McDonalds

9 Rose Crescent, Cambridge. Tel: 01223 303020

- Internet access.

- Salads & deli sandwiches.

- Traditional menu.

- Spacious & clean.

- Regular promotions.

"Now run by the efficient Karl Hubbard and team. The internet access is a great service at this ever popular brand leader. Browse the Web whilst enjoying a latte and a new deli sandwich in spacious and comfortable surroundings."

173

174

175

The Dyke's End

8, Fair Green, Reach. Tel: 01638 743816

Superior quality, country pub food utilising seasonal and local produce. 5 well kept real ales. "We are not a pub restaurant! We are a village pub with 2 beautiful dining rooms."

"The Dyke's End is regarded as one of the best pubs in the region. An excellent venue for outstanding cuisine in wonderful surroundings."

176

178

Scandinavia Coffee House

30 Abbeygate Street, Bury St Edmunds. Tel: 01284 700853

A wide selection of teas and coffees.

Light lunches.

Mouthwatering home-made cakes.

"A delightful coffee house located in the historic area of Bury. You are bound to be tempted by the Danish open sandwiches and the aroma of freshly baked cakes."

Authentic Thai cuisine served both lunchtimes and evenings. Quality wines and genuine Thai beer.

Thai Light

33 High Street, Halstead. Tel: 01787 477577

"A seventeenth century, classical English building with a genuine Thai interior. Lots of authentic furniture gives a true flavour of the Orient, matched only by the food!"

179

180

"A grade II listed pub named after the tree in the garden, with 2 magnificent inglenook fireplaces. Now run by Sue & Sean who have brought a touch of Dublin to Suffolk!"

"A pretty, sixteenth century building which has been beautifully refurbished. A very family orientated establishment with a large beer garden."

"Step back in time to this beautifully kept, sixteenth century smugglers inn boasting warming fires in winter and a year round welcome to match! Excellent for all types of function."

"Fresh and appealing are descriptive words that best suit this beautiful venue! Excellent food, lovely views and some stimulating walks too."

"Nice to see a privately owned hotel of such quality. A delightfully historic sixteenth century building that houses 11 en suite rooms with great facilites and services. Lovely food at reasonable prices and a super place for a party or function."

183

Kings Arms

The Green, Shouldham. Tel: 01366 347819

Come and enjoy our relaxing atmosphere, with intimate dining areas where you can treat yourself to real home-made foods including our famous sticky toffee and spotted dick desserts.

"This charming village pub is now run by Ben Hall. Situated on The Green, it provides good, country cooking in the most relaxing of surroundings."

Orchard Tea Gardens

45 Millway, Grantchester. Tel: 01223 845788

Come and visit our tranquil gardens in historic Grantchester. Sample from a vast range of cakes and home baked items and you must try our classic cream tea. If you want a party or function with a truly unique venue, give us a call.

"New manager, Pauline has recently taken-over and is not upholding, but improving standards at this delightful orchard venue. Come and sample a piece of history, where time stands still."

184

Musgrave Arms

16 Apsley End Road, Shillington. Tel: 01462 711286

- Corporate events & weddings.

- Excellent home cooked food.

- 1 acre of land perfect as a centre piece for a marquee.

- petanque area, why not try your hand?

"Quaint and cosy with a real fire. The separate dining room is a pleasant spot where you can enjoy good food, beautifully presented."

King William IV

High Street, March. Tel: 01354 653378

Enjoy diverse tastes, from fresh market salmon to beef in black bean sauce. Families will appreciate our fully enclosed patio, ideal for balmy summer evenings!

LIVE MUSIC & DISCOS   **3 EN SUITE ROOMS**

"The hard work that Dick & Sheila have put in is evident. Now boasting 3 excellent en suite bedrooms, this location is ideally placed, just 1/2 a mile from the town centre."

186

The Priory Roast

High Street North, Dunstable. Tel: 01582 661530

We offer an extensive menu of home-made food, from simple but tasty snacks to superb, succulent steaks. Come to our popular carvery on Wednesdays and Sundays, but book first to avoid disappointment!

"A lovely building that has been restored to its former glory by Russell & Debbie. There's a fabulous new menu and a carvery that has to be sampled. Nice beer garden too."

The Mother Red Cap

80 Latimer Road, Luton. Tel: 01582 730913

OPEN ALL DAY

We serve a nice variety of home-made dishes and a full Sunday lunch featuring a choice of 3 roasts. We keep 3 real ales and provide regular live entertainment.

"Mike & Ken have transformed this friendly town pub and it now has the appearance of a country local. Warm atmosphere and a lovely new beer garden."

"Sited in a former public house, this atmospheric venue is 400 years old. Freshly refurbished to create a modern interior, yet retaining all its character."

"Now run by Sheila & Kevin who have added a warm and welcoming atmosphere to this picturesque village local. A superb large garden with a fully secure play area keeps the children happy."

The Bombay

77-79 High Street, Stevenage. Tel: 01438 314699

Exotic Bangladeshi, Indian
& Nepalese cuisine.
5 course gourmet menu
every Tuesday evening.
Fully licenced, with a good
range of Indian beers.

"The oldest Indian restaurant in Stevenage and now under new ownership. A fine, contemporary interior enhances the excellent menu."

Mama Rosa's Italian Ristorante & Pizzeria

3 North Street, Leighton Buzzard. Tel: 01525 375149

Come and enjoy the best in
Italian cuisine. Pizzas,
pastas and Mama Rosa's
fillet steak, all cooked to
order, as well as excellent
Italian wines and beers.

"A great family venue, ideal for dinner with friends or a romantic supper. In summer dine alfresco in the pretty water garden."

189

The Royal George

High Street, Stagsden. Tel: 01234 822801

You'll love our fine country fayre which focuses on seasonal and local produce, served both lunchtimes and evenings.

"A quaint village pub that dates back to 1827 and is set in an acre of land. Enjoy wonderful food from French chef Alain, after which you can have a relaxing stroll in the grounds. Perfect for families with a nice children's play area."

The Horse & Groom

15 High Street, Clapham. Tel: 01234 217502

We serve a varied menu of wholesome dishes both lunchtimes and evenings, including some excellent daily specials and a superb Sunday roast.

BOOKING ADVISABLE

"A family run and family welcoming seventeenth century pub, formerly a coaching inn with lots of original features, as well as an award winning garden. Chef Aaron Reynolds has created a wonderful menu utilisng local produce."

191

The Castle

17 Newnham Street, Bedford. Tel: 01234 353295

We serve a menu of freshly cooked dishes, with something to suit everyone.

Our desserts are irresistible!

Real ales, wines and accommodation too.

"Now owned by Tom and Joanne, this rural pub has a feel of the countryside. The beer garden is much improved and features new patio heaters."

Il Forno

48 High Street, Baldock. Tel: 01462 491110

We serve a wonderful menu of authentic Italian cuisine, as well as an extensive list of Italian wines. We are renowned locally for our fresh fish dishes.

"New owner, Antonio Ciarvella, has done a wonderful refurbishment job and along with his food and wines, really has created a little corner of Italy."

192

193

"New managers Barry & Wendy Robinson have created a family orientated venue and a very welcoming atmosphere. Great fun for all the family."

"A traditional village pub now run by Sue Manning. The large garden with summer marquee and children's play area is a popular attraction for families."

194

The Cock Inn

25 Church Street, Gaminglay. Tel: 01767 650255

Tasty, freshly prepared home cooking; you have to try our superb cod in beer batter! There's lots to explore with lawned areas, a lovely beer garden, petanque pitch and a superb, wooden play area for kids.

NOW RUN BY JERRY & NICOLE

"Steeped in history, with a gorgeous inglenook fireplace. The enormous garden has hidden depths. Something for all the family without losing the traditions of a 'proper pub'."

"Probably one of the best all-round family destinations in the region. A fantastic garden and conservatory as well as a children's playground."

196

"*Ryan & Claire Kirk run what is really a village pub, on the edge of a town centre!*"

"*An idyllic, thatched village free house, now owned by the vastly experienced Robert & Marion Lowrie. Full of character, with an elegant restaurant and delightful garden.*"

197

"Richard & Caroline have lovingly refurbished this charming olde worlde pub. They serve excellent food and have successfully created a truly family atmosphere."

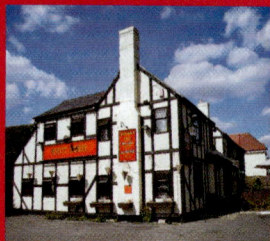

"A fascinating experience, with a spectrum of dishes from classic English bar snacks like stuffed mushrooms, to a taste of the Orient with spicy meat dumplings."

198

"Shaun Gilder has revitalised this charming, grade II listed, eighteenth century inn and has retained many original features. Nestling beneath Grimsthorpe Castle, the rooms are lovely and the menu very interesting."

"Beautifully refurbished, the Gordon Arms is now a fine venue for relaxed dining. Manager Oliver Darling has not only created a relaxed atmosphere, but ensures efficient service and attention to detail at all times."

200

We serve high quality a la carte and bar menus.

Real ales and fine wines.

Fully equipped children's play area.

All functions welcomed.

34 Manor Road, Folksworth. Tel: 01733 240258

"A delightful seventeenth century free house which has been fully refurbished to a very high standard. Now under the ownership of Graham Bond, who along with his co-chef has created a superb menu. This is not to be missed!"

201

202

203

The Bulls Neck

Penny Hill, Nr. Holbeach. Tel: 01406 422154

We serve a great variety of food on our bar and a la carte menus, as well as a selection of popular daily specials and a wonderful 3 course Sunday lunch, with desserts that are just too tempting!

"Now run by Richard Harris who has refurbished throughout. Lots of character with a warm and friendly ambience. Well worth a visit."

Plough Inn

Main Road, Deeping St. Nicholas. Tel: 01775 630260

Excellent English food, with daily specials and a fantastic Sunday roast! We also welcome both families and all types of function.

"Located in the centre of one of the longest villages in England, this grade II listed pub has been beautifully refurbished to its former glory by new owner, Angela Du Feu."

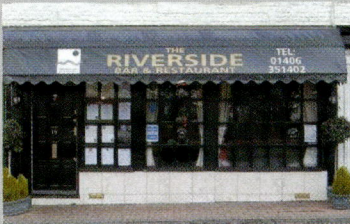

"Boasting a lovely venue beside the Swing Bridge, this venue is now run by Christine & Stuart, who have created a friendly environment for customers both old and new."

"New owners, Robert & Chris Meek have already gained a 'Casque Marque' award. They have elegantly refurbished the large restaurant and offer full function facilities for private parties."

205

Wait For The Waggon

13 Great North Road, Wyboston. Tel: 01480 212443

We serve a full menu of international dishes and a range of home-made desserts. Sunday roasts, tasty snacks and a children's menu

LARGE BEER GARDEN

"A very friendly pub with good parking and ideally positioned for access to the A1. Now under new ownership and carefully restored to incorporate a safe play area for children within a secure garden."

The Angel Inn

St Osyths Lane, Oundle. Tel: 01832 273767

Come in and sample our broad menu of home cooked fayre, featuring our daily specials board. Sunday lunches and quality real ales.

"Dennis Horgan is the proud owner of this traditional, old pub and has been established for ten successful years. Renowned locally for the quality of both his food and his ales."

206

"A historic venue and listed. Located next door to the poet John Clarke's (1793-1864) house, with much of his work on display. An excellent example of an English village pub."

"Set in the heart of the Fens, this fifteenth century, olde worlde establishment has abundant character and is now owned by Jane and Kevin, who have created a lovely ambience. Well worth a visit."

207

Victoria Inn

52 Ouse Walk, Huntingdon. Tel: 01480 453899

We are proud to announce our re-opening in January 2006 after an extensive refurbishment. Come and see the differences, including our new non-smoking restaurant.

"Phil and Teresa have just completed a painstaking refurbishment and serve superb, English food. The atmosphere is friendly and this is a lovely clean and fresh environment in which to relax."

Green Man

East Street, Colne, Huntingdon PE28 3LZ

Tel: 01487 840368

"Phil and Teresa (see above), serve a good and varied menu of home cooked food, real ales and fine wines. They now have an elegant, separate restaurant and are hosts to two beer-festivals annually. An excellent venue for functions."

"Owner, Felix Chow has created a little piece of China here! Authentic food, with some interesting and unusual dishes. You must try the Chinese Great Wall wine."

"A bright, modern, free house which has been totally refurbished to create a stylish, triple level, eating area. Wine, dine and then dance the night away at Lesters night club."

"A lovely old, eighteenth century free house, run by Peter and Virginia Robinson. Full of character and boasting a superb air conditioned restaurant serving an imaginative menu."

"New tenants, new menu! Glen & Maxine have put their own stamp on the place and we're sure you'll notice the difference. Nice food in an informal atmosphere."

"Within the Duke of Bedford's 'Model Village', this pub boasts one of the most extensive menus, with over 100 items to choose from. Two pretty beer gardens, with one securely enclosed for children, as well as an animal area."

"Very homely, where the presentation is first class and the staff are both efficient and courteous. It really is 'home from home'."

211

579-581 Lincoln Road, The Triangle, New England, Peterborough.

Restaurant Tel: 01733 552211 Takeaway Tel: 01733 319988
www.shanghaigarden.co.uk

A la carte evening menu Friday-Wednesday. Buffet bar Thursday evening & daily set lunches.

WE SPECIALISE IN FRESH FISH DISHES

"Classic Oriental cuisine with a warm and friendly ambience. Ideal for parties of all types. They also provide a full outside catering service."

Unit 1, White Hart Market Place, Spalding.

Tel: 01775 719012

www.shanghaigarden.co.uk

Full a la carte evening menu Friday-Wednesday. Buffet bar Thursday evening & daily set lunches. Separate function room.

"A new sister restaurant with elegant decor that is fully air conditioned. A grade II listed building, with lovely beams and fireplaces which oozes history."

*"A great family venue, dating to the 1600s, that has been
recently refurbished by Shirley and Alan, who now provide
excellent disabled facilities."*

*"Great food, from an excellent chef. The 3 course lunch is
superb and very good value at £22. You must try their home
baked bread service too!"*

Winteringham Fields Restaurant

Silver Street, Winteringham. Tel: 01724 733096

Restaurateurs Restaurant of the Year 2003
2 Michelin Stars and 5 AA Rosettes

Our world renowned restaurant serves European Modern cuisine of the highest standard in a homely yet stylish dining room. All dishes are prepared from local produce and include daily fresh fish and game in season from local shoots.

7 INDIVIDUALLY DESIGNED LUXURIOUS BEDROOMS

"A marvellous, multi award winning venue where attention to detail is evident in every facet of the business. Superb food, utilising the best local produce resulting in stunning cuisine."

"New owner, Gavin Richards has beautifully refurbished not only the building, but the menu too! Close to The Viking Way walk this is an ideal place to eat, drink and stay."

"The vastly experienced Martin & Irene have created an outstanding menu, as well as a warm and family welcoming atmosphere and have also lovingly restored the beer garden."

"Now run by Phil & Amanda Brierley who have made many improvements to this traditional pub as well as introducing new menus. The carvery is very good and excellent value. All in all, a super venue for families."

"Chef du Patron, Benjamin Edwards, has 25 years experience and you can be assured of an outstanding dining experience. A warm ambience enhanced by a roaring fire in winter and for summer there's a lovely beer garden."

218

"Mark Broadbent is the new Chef du Patron of this elegant yet comfortable and relaxing restaurant, situated in the 'Fortescue Arms'. This is an ideal venue for functions"

"May the spice be with you! A new and interesting venue for Lincoln, boasting a super riverside position."

"A delightful new venue for Brigg, now owned and run by George & Gillian Newcombe. The experienced chef, Lisa Wood, has created a menu of her own creations. Well worth a visit."

"A family owned, grade II listed free house, ideally situated close to the train station, There's a fantastic function room that is ideal for weddings and parties. CAMRA commended for their real ales."

220

The Beach Bar
High Street, Sutton On Sea. Tel: 01507 441453

Good bar menu of freshly cooked food, with the accent on fish. Families are welcome, functions are catered for and we have full disabled facilities.

"Fully refurbished by the new owners, The Beach Bar has something to offer the whole family. Children have their own room with activities, whilst parents will enjoy the conservatory and the picturesque patio complete with sea views."

The George & Dragon
High Street, Hagworthingham. Tel: 01507 588255

Food served from noon till 9pm, including a bar menu, daily specials and on Sundays our famous carvery. Children have their own menu and a new Adventure Playground!

"Jackie & Martin have made this into a fabulous family orientated pub. Lovely country views, great walks and just a short drive from the coast ."

221

"A grade II listed building dating to 1725, now owned by John & Carol, who have lovingly restored the hotel to its former glory. A wonderful base from which to explore this historic town and enjoy many famous walks."

"Award winning chef, Steven King, and his partner Lianne oversee this charming, traditional local that dates back to 1845. Close to RAF North Cotes, the pub boasts a host of fascinating aviation memorabilia."

"A very popular venue where Giovanni ensures that you have a memorable eating experience. Great views from the balcony, of this historic cathedral city."

"Beautifully refurbished by local businesman and famous artist, Mr Yeung. A superb venue, with many of his paintings adorning the walls. He will even show you his entry in the Guinness Book of Records!"

224

The Ship Inn
20 High Street, Billinghay. Tel: 01526 860756

We are proud of our high quality English food and you must try our superb Sunday carvery! We specialise in functions and can provide outside bars too.

"Enjoy excellent traditional English food in the elegant restaurant, or utilise the fabulous function room, complete with bar, dance floor and DJ booth."

The White Swan
Newark Road, Torksey Lock. Tel: 01427 718653

You'll enjoy our jovial atmosphere which is just perfect for sampling good beers, wines and lovely home cooked food.

"This charming riverside venue is now run by 2 excellent chefs, John & Denise Cross who serve an array of their own interesting creations."

226

"Under the ownership of the Moore family, this beautifully refurbished free house is on the intersection of the rivers Trent and Idle. It now has a pretty patio garden and plans include a new restaurant and full conference facilities."

"A beautiful, waterside location where owners, Phil and Carol Smith and their highly skilled team create an array of fine dishes."

The Durham Ox

Main Road, Thimbleby. Tel: 01507 526871

Come and enjoy a real country pub and sample a diverse, freshly cooked menu, real ales, wines and a beer garden that is ideal for all families.

"A real country welcome from previous managers and now tenants, Chrissie & Dean. Their large, separate restaurant is ideal for all types of functions."

The Homestead

Canwick Avenue, Bracebridge Heath, Lincoln. Tel: 01522 546400

An extensive menu is served from:

Noon to 10pm Monday-Saturday,

noon to 9.30pm Sunday.

Real ales and fine wines.

Families welcome.

Garden and play area.

"This grade II listed pub is a stately building with wonderful stained glass windows, ornate coving, eaves and an imposing staircase. New manager Karen Dobbs has created a really friendly environment to complement the magnificiently refurbished interior."

228